"Everyone needs to use the brilliant affirmations
for prosperity in *Secrets to Lifelong Prosperity*.
I love them *and so will you!*"

—Mark Victor Hansen, Bestselling Author,
The One Minute Millionaire and *Chicken Soup for the Soul*

About This Book

Secrets to Lifelong Prosperity, 64 Timeless Truths That Will Change Your Life, presents the Universal Laws of Prosperity together for the first time in one effective program.

The Universal Laws of Prosperity are time-tested principles based on natural law. When you understand and apply these powerful Prosperity Laws to your life, you can fully create, share, and enjoy personal and financial abundance.

Each Universal Law comes in the form of an uplifting affirmation with instructions to get your life moving toward prosperity and success every day.

Following each affirmation is a quick but powerful activity that puts your knowledge of the Universal Law into action. These activities bring you real, positive change and help you experience each Prosperity Law at a deeper level.

You don't have to sift through pages of theory or anecdotes; the simple and effective affirmations and activities give you an immediate understanding of the power and meaning of these principles and help you put them to work right away. More than a reading tool, this unique book was designed to be experienced.

You may have read other personal growth books with little success. Perhaps you were inspired for a week or two and then moved on without enacting any real change. But *Secrets to Lifelong Prosperity* contains powerful steps that can lead you through a transformational journey.

(Excerpt from page 21)

Secrets to

Lifelong Prosperity

64 Timeless Truths That Will Change Your Life

Heidi Baer

HAR-MONEY™Cards©1991-2005 by Heidi Baer
HAR-MONEY™ is a Trademark of
Treasure Island Press
PO Box 6477, Portland, OR 97208

Visit our Web site at http://www.HarmoneyCards.com

Quantity discounts are available on bulk purchases of
Secrets to Lifelong Prosperity and the *HAR-MONEY™ Cards*
for reselling, subscription incentives, gifts, fund raising
educational, business, or sales promotional use.

For information, please contact our Special Sales Department at
Treasure Island Press
(800) 795-0770
Business@HarmoneyCards.com

Cover and Interior Book Design by Heidi Baer
Edited by Craig Kramer

Permissions appear on Page 297.

ISBN 0-9633697-8-4
Library of Congress Control Number: 2004096759
Printed in the United States of America
First Printing ©2005

Dedicated to

the creative spirit within us all

And now here is my secret,
a very simple secret:

It is only with the heart that one can see rightly;
What is essential is invisible to the eye.

—Antoine de Saint-Exupéry
From *The Little Prince*

Contents

10. Money and You (Continued)

One can never consent to creep

When one feels an impulse to soar.

—Helen Keller

Your Life as a Masterpiece

Have you ever wondered how Olympic ice skaters learn to dance gracefully across the ice? Have you marveled at how great artists create paintings so beautiful that they move people for centuries? How do virtuoso musicians effortlessly play their instruments and make music that touches your soul?

Master artisans feel an intuitive force working through them. Although they may or may not consciously understand how to harness this power, they instinctively use it for their highest forms of expression. By sidestepping their judgmental self-consciousness and allowing this higher energy to express itself, they slip into the flow, beauty, and rhythm of life.

Creating a great work of art is similar to creating an extraordinary life. Just like the artist who surpasses everyday standards to create a masterwork, we too can tap into a higher creative power that allows us to transcend limitations and surpass our expected standards.

Within us and all around us, this power (or creative intelligence) is a subtle yet natural force that we often overlook in our daily lives. But if we follow an individual path to prosperity, this creative intelligence will come to our aid.

When you learn to tap into this higher force, every breath you take gives you a fresh opportunity to turn your own life into a masterpiece.

The most beautiful thing
we can experience is the mysterious.
It is the source of all true art and science.

Albert Einstein

Prosperity Is Natural

Everywhere we look in nature, we can see evidence of immense abundance. Stars are innumerable, as are grains of sand. The universe is more vast than the human mind can comprehend.

The power that created this incredible cosmos also created you and me. We humans consist of the same intelligent energy that governs the rest of our earth and the entire universe. This loving energy is available to us all. We can tap into this force and use it to realize our full potential and to help others, creating the prosperous life and world that we desire.

We harness this great energy by first becoming aware of it. It is as natural as our own breath, and it is everywhere and in everything. This energy surrounds us like the ocean surrounds a fish. Indeed, it is the stuff of the universe.

Natural laws direct this force. For our purposes, we call them *The Universal Laws of Prosperity*. The Prosperity Laws have been passed down as success secrets throughout the ages. They make sense from a logical standpoint, and for many, they will also resonate as truth on a much deeper level.

We call these natural laws "secrets" because society generally teaches us to think in terms of lack and limitation. Thus, the wisdom presented by these success principles may at first seem foreign or unnatural. But once you become aware of the Universal Laws of Prosperity and begin to use them, a more prosperous and fulfilling life awaits you. This abundant life is your natural birthright.

Matter, Energy, and Reality

The world in which we live is actually made up of two worlds. These two worlds can be called the "seen" and the "unseen." The first is the one that we are all raised to believe in as reality. But it is within the second world that we truly find reality. This second world is completely invisible and difficult to perceive, so many people have trouble discovering that it exists.

We think that the "seen" world is all that there is because it registers directly with our senses: We can touch, taste, hear, smell, and see this world, so we believe that it must be real and that there is no more to it.

But there is much more. Modern science has introduced us to the molecular world, a world invisible to us. We know that everything is made up of atoms and molecules (and a lot of empty space). Atoms and molecules are in constant motion. We also know that atoms consist of even smaller particles, which behave like energy waves. Scientists have photographed these waves, trapping them in a single moment in one place and even in several places simultaneously. This energy is part of all the solid matter of our universe, including inanimate objects, plants, animals, humans, planets, and stars.

An oak tree, for example, is composed of innumerable molecules and atoms, the basic building blocks of all things. In its simplest state, the oak is matter and energy. The way the oak tree, or any solid matter, manifests itself depends on the placement and quantity of the molecules and atoms within it; the matter and energy of the oak are concentrated bits of specific information coming together in space and time.

The World Beyond Our Senses

All objects and sounds that we are able to perceive with eyes and ears come to us in the form of waves of energy. Our eyes are capable of receiving waves of a certain frequency range, which our brain interprets as sight. Our ears can receive another range of energy waves, which we interpret as sound. A sound wave pulsates through the medium of air, disturbing the air but not carrying the air with it. Visualize a wave moving through water or a field of grain.

The difference between something we see and something we hear is merely a difference in frequency. Although our perception is limited to certain ranges of frequency by our senses, other forms of energy can be received, measured and utilized with the help of various scientific instruments.

We trust our senses of sight, sound, taste, touch, and smell to confirm reality in our universe. Yet our senses do not discern much more than surface, or superficial, reality. As we know, solid matter is not entirely solid but made up of tiny particles of matter and energy. Through the understanding that our physical senses alone cannot give us a completely accurate picture of this world, we come to realize that much of the world must exist beyond what we can perceive.

Beyond our senses is the world of the "unseen." We have difficulty understanding this world because we are conditioned to experience "reality" as our limited physical world. But our physical world actually issues from this great, unseen force. This unseen force consists of an intelligent energy. It beats our hearts; it transforms an embryo into a full-grown human being; it keeps our entire universe in balance and harmony.

People have called the unseen force by many names. For our purposes, we will refer to it in a variety of ways, including "creative force," "higher power," "great spirit," and sometimes "God." For your own purpose, refer to it with any name that feels right to you. If you wish you can call it Fred.

Because we are an integral part of this unseen energy—and it, a part of us—we direct it with our thoughts, feelings, and beliefs. It is through working with this life energy that you can create a prosperous present and future.

The Amazing Power of Thought

Many scientists believe that thoughts are more than just words in your head: they are also units of energy that interact with the other energies of the universe and affect your physiology, attitudes, actions, and environment. What you think about yourself and the world helps to determine your reality and entire experience of life.

Core beliefs are clusters of similar thoughts about you and the world coupled with powerful feelings. Your core beliefs set the tone for the present moment. They influence every aspect of your life.

Core beliefs magnetize situations with similar energy, attracting circumstances and people according to their like and kind. Prosperous thoughts create an energy within and around you that naturally attracts wealth and success. Therefore, if you want to improve your life, begin by improving the quality of your thoughts.

Regular awareness of and attention to the Universal Laws of Prosperity integrates their qualities into your state of being, changing your energy. Daily practice of the Laws brings these qualities into your life in material form.

How to Use This Book

Secrets to Lifelong Prosperity, presents the 64 Universal Laws of Prosperity together for the first time in one effective program.

The Universal Laws of Prosperity are time-tested principles based on natural law. When you understand and apply these powerful Prosperity Laws to your life, you can fully create, share, and enjoy the abundance that is your birthright.

You may have read other personal growth books with little success. Perhaps you were inspired for a week or two but then moved on without enacting any real change.

However, this guidebook contains simple steps that can lead you through a transformational journey. It was not created just to be read; it was designed to be *experienced.* Confucius (559-471 B.C.) said,

> *I hear and I forget; I see and I remember;*
> *I do and I understand.*

Secrets to Lifelong Prosperity presents each Universal Law in the form of an uplifting affirmation with instructions to get your life moving toward prosperity and success each day.

Following each section is a quick but powerful activity that puts your knowledge of the Universal Law into action. These activities bring you real, positive change and help you experience each Prosperity Law at a deeper level.

You don't have to sift through pages of theory or anecdotes—the simple and effective affirmations and activities give you an immediate understanding of the power and meaning of these principles.

This unique approach to creating prosperity is designed to fit easily into your lifestyle. The program is flexible. You can work through it quickly, or you can take your time with each Prosperity Law. You might choose to read through the book first and go back to do the activities later. You might also wish to keep this guidebook nearby to refer to it often.

We begin this program by examining how our perceptions create our reality and the amount of prosperity we will accept into our lives. We also discuss the nature of true prosperity and review several effective methods for cultivating a mindset for creating joyful abundance.

We then talk about how to get in tune with the universal creative intelligence and how it operates in your life. Several activities help strengthen your relationship with your higher power as you learn to work with it to craft your life into a masterpiece. This leads to a discussion of prosperity and creating money from a spiritual standpoint.

Next, we explore the prosperity tools to design a vision of your perfect life. This section helps clarify what is important to you materially, as well as spiritually, and what is essential for your happiness. You also discover a unique method to define your true purpose and to integrate it into your life in harmony with your goals.

The book finishes by examining the five essential areas of life that need to be balanced in order to create true prosperity on all levels. In addition, we learn several effective methods for clearing and releasing negativity so our prosperous thoughts have room to flourish.

As you go through the following chapters, you will experience life as a rich and rewarding journey; then understanding of the Universal Laws will come to you naturally.

The Har-Money™ Cards

Secrets to Lifelong Prosperity was originally written as a companion manual to the HAR-MONEY™ *Cards*, which present the 64 Universal Laws of Prosperity on daily affirmation cards. *Secrets* can be enhanced by using the HAR-MONEY™ *Cards*, though each is designed to be effective whether used together or separately.

The HAR-MONEY™ *Cards* help you easily integrate the Prosperity Laws into your daily life. The front of each card displays one of the 64 numbered Prosperity Laws from this book, while the back of the card explains the law.

You can randomly choose one of the HAR-MONEY™ *Cards* out of the deck of 64. You may be pleasantly surprised to find that you often select the message you most need to hear for that day.

You can post the card in your immediate environment: on your computer keyboard, refrigerator, or automobile dashboard. If you like, carry the prosperity card with you as a reminder or touchstone to inspire you throughout the day. The next day, you pick a new card from the deck.

The HAR-MONEY™ *Cards* are simple to use, yet they provide wisdom and profound insights.

The numbers assigned to each Prosperity Law in *Secrets to Lifelong Prosperity* correlate with the numbers on each HAR-MONEY™ *Card* for easy cross-referencing. If you pick a card and would like to explore its Universal Law in more detail, you can easily look it up by its corresponding number in this guide.

Secrets expands on each Universal Law of Prosperity by dedicating a page or more to describing how the law works, followed by a simple activity that helps you understand the power of the law quickly and easily.

Because this book derives from the HAR-MONEY™ *Cards*, this book is, in essence, a HAR-MONEY™ *Guidebook*.

If you want more information about the HAR-MONEY™ prosperity cards and how they work, please visit http://www.HarmoneyCards.com or use the contact information on page 295.

Your Prosperity Journal

Find any kind of blank notebook, and label it "Prosperity Journal." You will use it to record your journey through these pages. This notebook will be your companion as you explore the Prosperity Laws, gain new insights, and respond to the activities. You can also use it to record your card of the day, write down coincidences that happen to you while you are learning the Prosperity Laws, and list the inspirational ideas that pop into your head.

Your Prosperity Journal is a treasure chest that reinforces your prosperity consciousness because it holds your special thoughts and uplifting ideas all in one place. Whenever you need a lift, you will be able look in your journal and get a prosperity boost.

We have designed the forthcoming *HAR-MONEY™ Prosperity Journal* with all this in mind. It is a guided journal that takes you through all the activities presented in *Secrets to Lifelong Prosperity*. It contains blank pages to record your answers and is sprinkled with inspirational quotes and additional insights to reinforce the material in this program. If you would like more information about the *HAR-MONEY™ Prosperity Journal*, use our contact information on page 295, or visit: http://www.HarmoneyCards.com/

1.

The Universal Laws
of Prosperity

Regardless of what language you speak,

your intent manifests through the word.

The word is not just a sound

or a written symbol.

The word is a force;

It is the power you have

to express and communicate,

to think,

and thereby to create the events in your life.

—Don Miguel Ruiz

Prosperity Law #1
My Words Have Power

Everyone knows that words are important. They constitute the primary form of human communication. They allow us to express ourselves and to reach and touch others. They influence individuals and entire societies, causing both to act in good and bad ways.

But words are even more important than all this, more powerful than most people realize. Words are energy. As such, they influence your perception of the world and embody the power of your intentions.

Thus, it is vital to think and speak in terms of what you want in your life, instead of what you do not want. Just as turning on a light dissolves darkness, calling out the positive dissipates struggle.

You become great by thinking great thoughts and by backing those thoughts with your words, energy, emotions, and actions. Nurture uplifting ideas in your thoughts and words, and watch your life transform.

You create much of your experience by the words you speak.
When you verbalize an idea, you send out energy telling
yourself and the universe of an intention,
which makes the idea more likely to come to pass.
Watch your words, and speak only of what
you would want to have in your world.

Affirmations

The word gives form to the unformed.
The greater the consciousness behind the word,
the more power it will have.
—Ernest Holmes

Look around you. Almost everything that you see that humans created was first born in the imagination. Much of *your* own reality is built from the thoughts, images, and feelings first created within you.

Negative thoughts and feelings tend to bring negative experiences to us. They often repeat themselves like a recording with a skip in it. To replace negative thought patterns with more productive thoughts, you can use an affirmation.

Affirmations are positive thoughts and words that you repeat to yourself in order to achieve the results you want. State them in the first person and present tense, and express what you want to manifest. For instance, "My body is strong" or "I am confident" or "I now have a job that I love." You say them as if they are your reality now.

Repeating the prosperity affirmations in this book with positive emotion helps you to think and speak in terms of what you want in your life, rather than what you do not want. Your thoughts and words affect the unseen force, so confidently affirm your dreams, and watch as they grow into reality.

If you have been negative for many years, be gently persistent, and allow for gradual change. Patience and time may be necessary to turn old patterns around.

Prosperity Law #2

Action Is the Active Ingredient That Transforms My Goals into Reality

A journey of a thousand miles begins with one step.
—*Lao Tsu*

Change begins with a decision. People who successfully change their lives for the better decide, without a doubt, to leave the old way behind and to commit truly to their transformation. It is the *decision* that motivates and energizes them.

Appropriate action—guided action performed with clarity and in harmony with your higher self—is the next step in the process of change. Reading gives you information about a new direction, and following through with appropriate action transforms that information into positive results.

In any sport or game, for example, to make a successful effort, one must follow through. In baseball, golf, or tennis, you can't just take a swing at the ball and stop short; the ball won't go far.

A book can provide a road map for you to follow, but you must step onto the road and begin walking to reach your destination.

You are at a crossroads. Will you commit to achieving your dreams? Will you truly commit to your lifelong prosperity?

Set out with clear goals and positive expectations;
then watch for guidance and take action.
Being courageous enough to act on your intuition
brings your goals into reality.

Taking Appropriate Action

Most people spend more time planning their weekly grocery list than planning their lives. Is it any wonder, then, that so many are unfulfilled?

Stop for a moment to consider your reasons for taking this journey and the results you are looking for. Ask yourself the following questions:

•*What changes do I want to create in my life?*

•*What benefits would I like to attain from reading this guide?*

•*What is stopping me from creating true prosperity right now?*

•*Am I willing to allow prosperity and abundance into my life?*

After considering these questions, ask yourself two more:

•*Are these results that I desire worth committing to?*

•*Am I willing to take action to make my dreams come true?*

Following Through

Secrets to Lifelong Prosperity presents fun and insightful activities that teach you to connect with the creative force and help you to use the Prosperity Laws more effectively. You can complete most of these activities by answering them quickly off the top of your head; your first impulse is usually best.

You may wish to read through *Secrets* once and then to go back and perform the activities during your second time through. But be sure to complete them for a fuller understanding of the Universal Laws. Doing the exercises takes only a few minutes and will tremendously enhance the results you are seeking.

Reading this book with a commitment to yourself is much more effective than reading without one. Decide now if you will choose to make a commitment to take action toward your success by following through with the activities in this guidebook and applying the knowledge.

If you wish to make this commitment, sign the contract on the next page, *My Commitment to Prosperity*. You will reap great rewards by choosing this path.

My Commitment to Prosperity

I, _____, am committing
to creating true prosperity
and to achieving my personal best in life.
I choose to believe in myself and in my dreams.
I expect and intend to create lifelong prosperity.

I, _____, commit to reading
and performing the activities in this Guidebook.
I will stay open for positive guidance,
and I will take the appropriate actions
needed to create the results I desire.
I step away from old ways that no longer serve me,
and I declare myself free to prosper
for the highest good all.

Signed_____

Date_____

Whatever you can do or dream you can, begin it.
Boldness has genius, power, and magic in it.
Begin It Now.

Goethe

Until one is committed there is hesitancy,
the chance to draw back, always ineffectiveness.

Concerning all acts of initiative and creation,
there is one elementary truth,
the ignorance of which kills
countless ideas and splendid plans:
that the moment that one definitely
commits oneself, then Providence moves, too.

All sorts of things occur to help one
that would never otherwise have occurred.
A whole stream of events issues from the decision,
raising in one's favor all manner of unforeseen incidents,
meetings and material assistance,
which no one could have dreamed
would come her way.

—W. H. Murray

Striking the Match

> *It is better to light one candle*
> *than curse the darkness.*
> —Eleanore Roosevelt

You direct the creative force with your beliefs, intentions, actions, and expectations. Making a commitment to your success is a powerful action that propels the creative force in the direction of your dreams.

By confirming your decision to change and by committing to follow through with the appropriate actions, you are taking the first step toward lighting your prosperity candle.

If you haven't done so already, now is a good time to bring out your Prosperity Journal and begin using it. The journal helps to reinforce the prosperity concepts in this guidebook.

If you don't yet have a blank notebook to use as a Prosperity Journal or would like more information about it, see page 25 for details on how the journal will help you in your quest for lifelong prosperity and joyful abundance.

Prosperity Law #3
I See Myself in a New Light

From the time we are young, other well-meaning people fill our minds with their limiting and negative beliefs. They may have told us that life is a struggle, along with myriad other thoughts of difficulty. That is reality, we are told, and to expect anything more would label us dreamers. We may have never questioned the reality that those people handed us, and innocently enough, we are now living and dying by their rules.

Take a moment to look at the lives of those who taught you about reality. Are they happy, enjoying life and experiencing rich and rewarding relationships? If not, we cannot really blame them for passing on poor information, as they could not teach us what they themselves did not know. But we can take matters into our own hands by building a self-image that is positive and a belief system that supports us.

Would you like to harness your personal energy and use it to experience joy, purpose, and prosperity? You will attract wonderful experiences by adopting the Universal Laws of Prosperity and transforming your energy. No matter what your history, you can create a new positive future.

Learn to flow with the river of life. If life is a struggle, you are swimming against the current.

Just because your life has been a certain way in the past
doesn't mean it must be the same in the future.
The future can be different. You can make it different.
You can change.

Do Something Different

Are you happy, or are you feeling frustrated and dissatisfied? Can you imagine a life filled with joy? Many people cannot. They work at jobs they don't like, struggle with their finances, and are always ready to fill your ears with a list of complaints about what went wrong that week.

Consider this:

If you do what you've always done,
you'll get what you've always gotten.

If you do what other people are doing,
you'll get what other people are getting.

To get something different altogether,
you must do something altogether different.

You are forging your own path to prosperity, so prepare to do things in a completely different way.

Prosperity Law #4
There Is Good in Everything That Happens to Me from Now on

Have you ever heard this saying: "It is always darkest before the dawn"? This means that you often reach your darkest or lowest point before the sun breaks through with the answer that heals and transforms you.

The universe will let you know if you are out of balance by allowing a crisis to appear which finally causes you to find new answers and to do things differently. When the pain of staying the way you are becomes greater than the discomfort of making necessary adjustments, you are primed for transformation.

No matter what happens, your experiences are leading you to greater success. Our personal challenges make us stronger. When we are lost in suffering, pain is the warning sign that alerts us to trouble. Listen to the message that pain has to offer.

When you choose to believe that everything always works out for the best, you will turn adversity into opportunity. If you concentrate on the hidden good in tough situations, you will move through them quickly and receive unexpected blessings.

A Quitter Never Wins and a Winner Never Quits

Any fact facing us is not as important
as our attitude toward it,
for that determines our success or failure.
—Norman Vincent Peale

Successful people are not people who have never seen failure—quite the contrary. They merely keep going when times get tough.

Successful people fail all the time, but they fail with a different attitude. It is said that it took Thomas Edison 10,000 attempts to invent the electric light bulb. When someone asked Edison how he could continue on after having failed so many times, he replied, "Nonsense! I never failed. I have merely discovered 9,999 ways *not* to make a light bulb!"

You can't always tell when you're about to succeed, but giving up is a sure way to fail. There are millions of stories of people who gave up when success was just around the corner, only they didn't know it at the time.

Katherine Hepburn once quipped, "When you fall down, just pick yourself up, dust yourself off, and start off again!"

Gather strength in times of darkness. Look at each experience as a valuable learning tool. Follow the Universal Laws of Prosperity, and patiently allow the tides to turn in your favor.

Take a moment to think back to a time when you were tempted to quit but did not—and met with success as a result. Is there a situation in your life now that requires a bit more persistence? *Record your responses in your journal.*

Prosperity Law #5
I Choose Thoughts That Support My Prosperous Future

Since you help choose the future with your thoughts, wouldn't it be wise to choose thoughts that you would like to see manifested in your life? Choosing prosperous thoughts is a habit that you can develop over time. If you are used to poverty thinking, you will probably need to nudge yourself in the other direction.

Become aware of your thoughts and attitudes and the effect they have on you. If you suddenly experience a sinking feeling out of nowhere, ask what you were just telling yourself. Did you entertain discouraging thoughts? What kind of energy did they create for you?

Negative thoughts waste energy that you could use to move ahead. Negative thinking stops you from taking action. Choosing to believe in your dreams gets you much farther in life. Instead of thinking about why something cannot be done, think about why it is possible.

Poverty Thoughts? Prosperity Thoughts?
Each carries different energies and reaps different results.
Realize that you choose the future
each moment with your thoughts.
When you choose prosperous thoughts,
you choose a prosperous life.

The World of Possibilities

Open your mind to the possibility that there are realities other than the one you may have been told was true. When you decide to move beyond the reality created by the limiting beliefs imposed upon you as a child, you rise above the masses and move towards a life of your own making.

Each time you envision yourself becoming greater, discipline your mind to leave behind the discouraging reasons why your dreams are not possible. Think, instead, of the reasons why they can easily be so.

For instance, if you want a particular job or position, rather than thinking about the competition or the difficulty of getting a good job, say to yourself something like, "A company exists now which is just right for me and needs all the talents I possess."

You can add all the particulars, such as a great income, a nice boss, a good location. Because the truth is that the perfect position *is* waiting for you. By opening your mind to this possibility, you draw it into your life. A Buddhist adage states, *That which you are seeking is causing you to seek.*

According to Universal Law, you are not given a desire without a way to fulfill that desire. Your dreams to move forward in life are holy because they act as your compass to reaching your full potential. When you become all that you are meant to be, you fulfill life's plan for you, and you raise the vibration of the entire universe. When you look at life in terms of possibilities, the universe supports you, and the result is that you are more likely to discover and travel the path to your dreams.

Let us say that you live in a town of one million people and that you are looking for a job. Odds are terrific that at least one out of that million will have the perfect position for you. Realistically, many positions are likely available that will be more than satisfying. Once you recognize this fact, the next step for you is to connect with the people who are holding these opportunities in their hands. And this is where your prosperity principles come in.

When you follow the Universal Laws of Prosperity, you make room for miracles to occur in your life. The universe finds magical ways to bring you what you desire. Seemingly miraculous coincidences occur to show you that you are on the right track and to put you face to face with your dreams.

When you look at your situation in terms of what is possible, visible and invisible roads open up for you. You may get an idea to call someone that you haven't spoken to in a while. Or you might have a chance meeting in the street, leading to your perfect job.

Prosperity can come to you in an infinite number of ways as long as you stay open to the possibilities and don't limit yourself by thinking negatively. Just follow the Universal Laws, and allow the path to open up in the perfect way. When you raise your personal energy to vibrate at a higher level, you attract higher energies into your experience, and you'll be amazed at the synchronicities that occur.

Think about one or more times when an unusual coincidence opened up doors and new vistas for you.

Record this memory in your Prosperity Journal.

The Gap

The Gap is a place where the discouraging ideas of the mainstream fade away, a place where your positive dreams and goals are possible. Here you leave behind all the people with negative attitudes and self-defeating advice; their rules for life are no longer in effect. When you are in the Gap, you are inspired to go confidently in the direction of your heart's desires. A new set of rules applies in this world of prosperity.

In the Gap, you sense that a power greater than yourself is watching out for you and is completely on your side. This power wants you to achieve your life's goals for the good of all. Follow the Universal Laws of Prosperity, and you cannot go wrong.

You enter the Gap by seeing only the world of possibilities and by dropping all negative expectations. When you slip through the Gap, you raise your personal frequency to a level that is in tune with the universe. Because of this, you will notice things falling into place.

No longer do you shut yourself off from life's magic. Events begin to go your way. You find yourself in the right place at the right time, meeting the right people in amazing ways, and you discover a life that works out in your favor.

Activity: *Slipping Through the Gap*

When you slip into the Gap, you become conscious of your unlimited potential in life. Remember that in this new world, you let go of negative ideas and step into the world of all possibilities.

Envision the Gap to be the size of a rabbit hole about five feet in front of you. Mentally slip through this hole, similar to the way Alice slipped through the rabbit hole in *Alice in Wonderland*. Actually see yourself climbing through this imagined opening, head first. Once you have come all the way through to the other side, know that, although this other world looks the same, something is different. Negative expectations are now inert. The only things you allow here are your positive possibilities.

See yourself in a world where your dreams are within reach. Take into serious consideration why your dreams can truly become your reality. Allow yourself to think only in terms of what is possible.

When you are in the Gap, you open the channels to prosperity. You raise your vibration and attract new positive circumstances into your life.

Next time you notice yourself drifting along a path of negativity, grab hold of yourself, and remember to slip into the world of all possibilities.

Record your experience of slipping through the Gap in your journal.

There are no ordinary moments.

—Dan Millman

2.

Prosperity in the Present Moment

People in our society often hurry from one project to the next, never stopping to notice the fullness of the present moment. They think that happiness is a destination they will reach sometime in the future. They can't be happy now because they tell themselves, "I need to lose weight," "I don't have enough money," "I'm too old," "I'm too young," or "I haven't found my soul mate."

Rather than rushing to get to the end of *Secrets to Lifelong Prosperity*, enjoy this process of self-discovery while you learn the Universal Laws of Prosperity. Look for the value in each moment, regardless of where you are or where you tell yourself you *should* be.

Surrender your will or impatience by trusting that when you lay the groundwork in the present, the creative force will take care of the rest. By doing the footwork and leaving the results to a higher power, you begin to create a life of joyful abundance right here and now.

Prosperity Law #6
Time Presents Me with the Perfect Answers

When you notice yourself rushing to your destination, try to stop and come into the present moment. Take time to soak in the awareness that you are always in the right place at the right time. Respect the process of growth, and understand that a greater force that creates with perfect timing is at work in your life.

Everything that has happened up to now has brought you to this place. You've acquired the lessons and experiences you needed; otherwise, they would not have been in your life.

Trust that your life is unfolding as it should, whatever your circumstances. Know that as you begin to believe in your dreams, you draw them nearer. Allow the answers to come to you naturally as you steadily walk the path towards personal prosperity. Become aware of the true perfection of your everyday life.

Time is the substance with which you sculpt your life.
Be secure in the knowledge that when the time is right,
you will see your dreams come true.
The universe is rearranging itself for you right now.

The Hare and the Tortoise

One day a hare decided to antagonize the local tortoise by challenging him to a race. The hare figured he had an easy victory on his hands and began taunting the tortoise the minute the race began. He toyed with the tortoise as he ran circles around him and soon raced far ahead, leaving the tortoise in the dust.

When the hare could no longer see the tortoise behind him, he stopped for some carrot juice and took in some other distractions. Finally, the hare became sleepy and lay down for a nap.

All the while, the tortoise kept on his slow and steady pace. And a funny thing happened on the way to the finish line. As the hare chased rainbows in his sleep, the tortoise stayed on his path. To the surprise of all, the tortoise crossed the finish line first! The hare arrived at the finish line a bit later, disoriented and, not to mention, last.

And the moral of the story is…

Hares start activities quickly and easily but with no real focus on the goal. They impatiently anticipate the finish line because they believe deep down that "there" is somehow better than "here." That is why they are in such a hurry to get "there." Unfortunately, "there" does not exist; we only have the "here"—*and now.*

The hare believes that reaching his external goals will bring him lasting happiness. But even if he gets them, satisfaction lasts only a fleeting moment before his attention goes somewhere else to try to make him happy. The hare never really gets "there," even if he does cross the finish line.

In fact, it isn't the goal that the hare really wants at all. He wants the *feeling* that he thinks attaining the goal will give him. He believes the common illusion that something *outside* of him can make him permanently happy.

But in truth, the feeling of happiness he seeks comes from *inside* of him. Once the hare understands this, he will take the time to reflect on what he needs to change *within* in order to experience true happiness, success, and prosperity.

Ultimately, the hare must become aware of the intangible qualities or feelings that he wants to experience inside of him— as opposed to merely chasing the material goals that he mistakenly believes will make him happy.

If he does this, his dreams and goals will come to him naturally and in the perfect way. He may even discover that his real goal is different from what he initially imagined— and he may find greater happiness as a result.

The true goal is the internal experience you seek—
the feeling you believe the achievement will bring.

Your goals will come to you in the perfect way when you are poised and confident. You have no need to rush, grasp, or feel anxious, for you attract what you are.

Confidence is *knowing* you will get to the finish line eventually, like the tortoise. In the meantime, "now" is also wonderful, because you are in tune with life.

Success is enjoying the essence of every moment.

Prosperity Law #7
I Fully Experience Each Moment

The rare moment is not the moment
when there is something worth looking at
but the moment when we are capable of seeing.
—Joseph Wood Krutch

At this instant you possess the greatest gift you can ever receive—a gift more precious than the most valuable jewels on earth. This gift cannot be taken from you as long as you live. If you use this gift wisely, you will become prosperous beyond your wildest dreams. This gift is the gift of the present.

When you discover the power of the present moment, you become more receptive to the abundance all around you. You do not need to search outside yourself for the golden key to joy, inner peace, or prosperity. You must learn to be peaceful and content in this moment so that you can connect with the creative force to manifest and truly appreciate the riches in your life.

You hold the keys *within you* to true prosperity, and you have great resources at hand to transform your life. These keys and resources are here, now, in this present moment. This moment holds all that you have, all that you are, and all that you are to become.

This is the only moment in which you have power.
The past is done, and the future depends on
the choices you make now. Experiencing life
as rich and rewarding in each and every moment
leads to a more prosperous future.

Activity: *Being in the Present*

Stop for a moment, and take in your surroundings one at a time. Take note of where you are, the time of day or night, what is happening around you, and what you are feeling right now. Do not resist anything, just notice. Think about the month, day, and year and what lies beyond your present scope of awareness (where you are in your neighborhood, what state or country you are in, which part of the world, and so on).

You are not going anywhere right now, so let go of any feelings of stress or pressure. You are just pausing to be in the moment. Listen to the sounds around you. What is happening right now? What are you feeling? Take in a deep breath and become aware of your breathing.

The more you can relax and experience the moment, the more you become aware of the creative force. The creative force is *Now*. It is the wind in the trees. It is the sunshine and the night sky. It is the beating of your heart and every heart on this planet. It is your dreams and inspirations.

Do this activity as often as you wish. These are moments frozen in time, where you stop racing toward the future and fully take in the present.

Recording your experience of this activity in your journal, as well as the time, date, and any other observations you have, will strengthen your awareness of the present moment and your understanding of the creative force.

Nature is too thin a screen;
The glory of the Omnipresent God
bursts through everywhere.
—Ralph Waldo Emerson

Prosperity Law #8
I Experience Happiness and Satisfaction from Within

We do not see things how they are,
we see things how we are.
—Anais Nin

If you can't fully enjoy and appreciate the present, you won't fully enjoy prosperity when it comes to you. Your achievements will be no more than temporary distractions from an inner sense of discomfort. In addition, you might repel good things that would have come your way naturally had you been in a space to receive them.

You may think an achievement, a job, or a relationship will make you happy, but how many times have you found that your happiness over something new didn't last? New possessions brought only fleeting pleasure, and soon you were on to the next goal, job, or relationship to make you feel good again. Instead of stopping to enjoy your prize, you were already looking to the future for satisfaction.

Here is an important yet often overlooked secret: Your mental, emotional, and spiritual states follow you around, no matter how much money you have, where you are, or whom you are with. You will always go back to your regular level of functioning eventually, no matter how wonderful or thrilling your new accomplishments. Consider this:

Whatever you feel before achieving your goal(s)
is how you will feel soon afterwards.

In other words, do not confuse the attainment of money or possessions with the attainment of happiness.

People are often disappointed when they reach the pinnacle of success, only to find that they still feel the same on the inside as they did before. This disappointment is frequently the catalyst that makes them finally realize that without attending to their inner peace and happiness, nothing outside themselves will make them feel good for very long. That realization often marks the beginning of a true and successful quest to find happiness and prosperity from within.

Happiness and satisfaction are not qualities
that depend on outer circumstances,
nor do they come from the future or the past.
Each moment is a magical experience when you realize
your fulfillment lies within.

Now Is the Time

The time is always *now*. You can learn to feel happy and fulfilled now. Once you truly understand that nothing external can give you lasting joy and happiness, you are on your way to discovering the keys to true prosperity.

When you find your joy from within, all that you do becomes a joy. You are in touch with your soul, you know what you want and what you need, and you have the strength to create it. You have a greater sense of self-worth, and you feel more deserving of prosperity. As a result, you feel good enough to give yourself the very best.

The Good News

Happiness is our state of optimal functioning. We were not created to trudge from one miserable moment to the next. Carrying that type of energy merely sets us up for failure. When we radiate happiness, we are poised for peak performance. Because of this, joy is our natural state.

Our emotions magnetize our experiences and events to us. When we are feeling good, our energy is flowing freely: We are vibrating at a high level, and we attract helpful and positive people and circumstances into our lives. In addition, we feel confident and optimistic—thus greatly increasing our potential for success.

The next two activities help you naturally attract joyful abundance.

Activity A: *My Treasures*

Begin to find more inner-happiness by appreciating the wonders in your life now. Discover what is *right* about the present moment.

List seven treasures in your life and the positive feelings you experience when you think about them. These treasures can be as simple as fresh air, a sunset, your capacity for self-expression, or the ability to love. Remember that your most valuable resources are here in the moment, within your reach.

Use the list below as an example, and record your treasures in your Prosperity Journal.

My Treasures:

1. The joy I feel when I smell the roses in my garden.

2. Gratitude for my good health.

3. The love I have for my friends, family, and pets.

4. The wonder and mystery of my creative imagination.

5. The sacred relationship with my Higher Self.

6. My enthusiasm for life.

7. A sense of inner peace.

When you look over your own list, do you experience feelings of joy? Can you see how nothing in your environment has changed since you started this list, only your awareness and perception of the goodness in your life? These thoughts *triggered* your joy, but ultimately, the good feelings came from inside you.

Joyful Abundance

Since you attract into your life what you focus on, it behooves you to learn how to generate positive emotions readily. That way you can easily draw in the good things coming to you.

Our world is made up of energy. Your emotions are charged with energy. Situations come into your life that resonate with the type of energy you are sending out.

To raise your energy level, you need to create a positive inner climate. When you vibrate at the frequency of joy, you attract prosperity and positive experiences. Fortunately, the universe is naturally set up to help you achieve happiness, because positive thoughts and energies are many times stronger than negative thoughts.

Activity B: *Joyful Abundance*

Try this activity now, and record your experience in your journal.

Close your eyes, and become aware of your feelings and emotions in this particular moment. Whatever they are—negative, positive, or neutral—experience them fully for a few minutes.

Next, choose a positive, uplifting thought, one that makes you feel light and joyful. You may ask yourself questions, such as, "Whom do I love?" "What is going well in my life right now?" "What do I love to do?" "Who loves me?"

You may also wish to think about one or more of your treasures that you listed in the last activity.

Once you have that uplifting thought, image, or feeling in mind, focus on it for a few moments, and allow the positive energy to build.

Stay with these good feelings until you are thoroughly soaked in them. Let a sense of well being replace whatever you were experiencing before, good or bad. When you successfully immerse yourself in a positive inner experience, your personal life energy vibrates at a higher frequency and you attract more abundance.

You may want to perform this activity at various times during the week to learn to come back to a place of inner peace and happiness no matter what is happening in your outer world.

The purpose of life is joy.

—*Dalai Lama*

3.

Focus on Prosperity

When award-winning ice skaters dance across the ice or when major league ball players are at bat, they are fully present and aware. If they allow their attention to wander, they are likely to falter or lose their step.

Focused concentration harnesses creative energy. Without focused awareness in the present, all the talent, practice, or preparation in the world might amount to nothing. Success happens in the here-and-now.

Your projections of future and past events are simply projections. Stepping out of the shadowy images of your mind and placing your awareness in the present moment bring you into contact with the great creative force.

If you notice that you spend too much time worrying about the past or the future, begin building yourself up. You can neutralize negativity by choosing an opposing positive thought and repeating it to yourself *with feeling* until you are confident of it.

When your mind is idle, occupy your thoughts with uplifting words. I like an affirmation made popular by Louise L. Hay:

All is well in my world.

Relax, be gentle with yourself, and patiently affirm prosperity. Allow your dreams to navigate your life.

Prosperity Law #9
What I Concentrate on Expands

A seed must go through a natural growth process if you want it to blossom. First, you follow the basic guidelines on how to plant, water, and nourish the seed, and you supply the appropriate environmental conditions. Then you wait. The plant will grow when it grows. If you become impatient and dig up the seed to look at it, you will have stalled the process of growth. But if you are patient, a flower will blossom and flourish. You do not make the flower grow. You trust the creative life force to do its job.

Your thoughts, words, and actions are like seeds that you sow in your garden of life. What you choose to focus on in every moment contributes to your experience of reality.

It is precisely because you can decide where to place your focus that your power exists in the present.

Focus on what you want, and allow the creative process to take care of the rest. When you follow the guidelines of this game called life, you can plant your own garden of dreams and watch it grow.

In life, what you concentrate on expands.
When you exercise a muscle, it becomes stronger.
Plant and nurture a seed, and it grows.
Thoughts you exercise on a regular basis will strengthen
and grow into reality.

Activity: *Removing Blocks to Prosperity*

Gently steer yourself towards prosperity by becoming aware of the type of energy you are sending out into the universe right now.

Negative thoughts and emotions repel prosperity. If your thoughts, beliefs, and emotions are not in harmony with what you really want to create, they will conflict with your goals and dreams, and cause you to struggle.

By identifying negativity and letting it go before it has a chance to take hold, you begin to neutralize and drain the power it has over you.

If at first you find it difficult to concentrate on prosperity, do not become discouraged. Abundance thinking is a gradual process. Just as you may have developed negative thinking habits over a period of time, positive habits must be developed over time, as well.

Answer these questions on paper separate from your journal:

• Where in my body do I carry negative feelings about money or scarcity? (Do you have tension in your neck or shoulders, or a sinking feeling in your stomach? Is there tightness in your chest or throat? Do you knit your brow or clench your jaw?)

• What specific thoughts do I harbor about prosperity, money, or my expectations of life in general?

• Can I imagine myself as a prosperous person?

• Do I think having a lot of money is bad?

Note: *The more you can accept and love yourself for having learned any self-defeating habits, the easier it will be to let go of them.*

Prosperity Law #10
I Am Creating My Life Anew

As you go through this program, remember that you are not trying to "fix" anything in your life. The past is gone; all you have is the here and now. You are moving forward. You are creating anew and undergoing a transformation.

You are building a new life of prosperity and clearing out the old, making it easier for new thoughts and beliefs to take root. Let go of the past—do not try to change it. Step into the future without fighting what is or what was.

When you repeat positive affirmations, you are creating a fresh start. If an affirmation does not feel real or true at first, do not worry: If it were already true, you wouldn't need to say it.

You must ignore outer appearances and hold fast to your vision. This is not always easy, but when you can do so, your circumstances will change. Allow your new reality to take hold gradually in your mind and emotions, and you will soon see it come to be in the outside world.

> *It is not necessary for your conscious mind*
> *to believe the prosperity statements at first.*
> *Nonetheless, you are creating change.*
> *When you repeat these affirmations with feeling,*
> *your subconscious mind picks up new beliefs*
> *and creates new experiences for you.*

We know what we are,
but know not what we may be.
—Shakespeare

Alchemy and Prosperity

Alchemy is the ancient practice of trying to transform lead into gold. Medieval scientists sat in makeshift laboratories in front of cauldrons, spending years attempting this task. For the wisest of alchemists, this outer process symbolized more than the transformation of metals; it was a purification of the spirit.

We have two basic emotions: love and fear. Fear is often the absence of love (just as darkness is the absence of light). If we equate lead to the emotion of fear, and gold to love, we can become spiritual alchemists. Our goal is personal transformation.

Since love and abundance are higher vibrations, when you open your heart to love, you open yourself to abundance. If you tighten your heart with fear or negativity, you lower your vibration and restrict the flow of abundance into your life.

When you recognize that you are feeling a negative emotion, notice where that feeling appears in your body and accept it with love. Do not suppress the feeling; do not judge it. Breathe, and let it flow through you, gently allowing that feeling to integrate.

Since negative emotions vibrate at a low frequency, they are dark and heavy, like lead. These feelings become painful and toxic when you try to withhold them. When you push your feelings down, they go into your subconscious and continue to cause trouble. Practice letting these negative emotions go, and accept and love yourself for having all your feelings.

Activity: *The Alchemy of Prosperity*

Try this activity right now with whatever you are feeling, and record your experience in your journal.

Close your eyes, and become aware of all the sensations in your body. Notice which areas feel dark, clogged, or heavy and which areas feel light. Try to *feel* rather than think. Relax, breathe, and accept anything you are feeling. Sit quietly for a minute or so.

Acknowledging and not resisting negative emotions help them to move through you faster and dissolve. Just remember to love yourself no matter what.

After you have experienced your feelings for a few moments, breathe in deeply, and release any sense of darkness, heaviness, or tension with your breath. Do this three or four times, or more if you wish.

At the same time that any dark energy is leaving your body, imagine that you are breathing in a magnificent golden light. Allow this light to flow into your torso and fill up your chest.

When you feel you are glowing with light, send the feeling of love from your heart area to all parts of your body. Breathe in and imagine your entire body radiating with the warm, rich, golden light, transforming any darkness to light. Permeate and surround yourself with this energy, and allow it fill you up and soak into every cell of your body.

Do not judge yourself while completing this activity. Just try it, and do the best you can. Use this activity whenever you want to lighten and clear your energy. Every little bit of light goes a long way.

What lies behind us and

what lies before us

are tiny matters

compared to what lies within us.

—Ralph Waldo Emerson

4.

Recognizing Your Personal Power

There is only one corner of the universe
you can be certain of improving,
and that's your own self.
—Aldous Huxley

The universe is a marvelous feedback system that reflects your innermost self back to you. This self is the core, or "essence," of your being and holds your hopes, dreams, and desires. It is also home to your intuition, or "gut feelings," and knows your true purpose in life.

Whatever you feel, think, and believe deep within you, will mirror back in your world on many different levels. Do you ever notice that when you feel really good, people light up in response? Your good feelings come back to you, and the world smiles. Events in your life seem to fall magically into place.

You express outwardly what you are on the inside, and the energy you send into the world returns to you like a boomerang. You can run, but you cannot hide from your true self.

In this chapter, we will continue with the process of recognizing our personal power and transforming our selves and our lives by claiming our power and taking personal responsibility for our own success.

Prosperity Law #11

I Take Responsibility for Making My Own Changes

We are taught that controlling our lives means we have to manipulate people and situations in the outer world. But no matter how hard we try, sometimes things do not work out the way we planned: We don't always get the job, the car, or the partner that we wanted so badly, and our lives at times feel out of our control. But with a simple switch in perception, we can focus back on the true source of our experience:

Our Selves.

Often we relinquish our personal power to outside forces, believing that we can do nothing to affect or change things in our lives. But in truth, we have much more power than we realize.

If you think about it, much of what you believe is happening *to* you is actually happening *from* you. Your surroundings react to *you*—what you are doing or thinking or feeling. Whatever you do or have is experienced, and even instigated, through how you are *be*-ing. Attend to your be-ing, and what you do and have will become more rewarding.

Your outer circumstances are a mirror of your inner world.
It is your responsibility to see that your life works out
the way you want it to. No one else can do it for you.
The power to change your life is within you.

Activity: *Taking Responsibility*

Think about a particular day in your life when you were feeling angry or irritable. Consider the reactions of those around you. Did they respond favorably or unfavorably to the energy you were emanating? Did events—both large and small—in your life seem out of your control? How do you think your negative mood influenced the day?

Next, remember a time when you were feeling more centered and grounded. Did people react more positively? Did your day go a bit more smoothly? Did you feel a sense of connection with your higher self?

Right now, check within to see if you are you blaming someone or something outside yourself for your difficulties. If you take responsibility and make a few healthy inner changes, do you see how you might turn the situation around?

Write your answers in your journal.

Prosperity Law #12
I Seek Approval from Within

You laugh at me because I'm different.
I laugh at you because you're all the same.
—Anonymous

People can only judge you from outer appearances. Thus, they may never get an accurate picture of who you are inside. To try to please others by acting chiefly in ways you think will garner approval is to cage your own soul.

This is not to say that we should ignore the needs of others. But following your heart is a thoroughly different issue (although the boundaries between these two issues can often seem unclear).

The only authentic way to live is by listening to your heart. Who you truly are on the inside will then shine through gloriously and radiantly.

When you follow the path of your heart,
others may disapprove of your direction or choices.
Remain true to yourself.
The only approval you really need is your own.

Activity: *Boldly You*

> *Once you decide who you are,*
> *nobody can define for you what you should be.*
> —Oprah Winfrey

Think of a time when you made a bold decision based on your own intuition. This is a time when you were true to yourself without fear of the judgment of others. Perhaps you decided to have your hair styled in a new way, stood up for something you believed was right, or took on a project with special meaning to you. Big or small, what matters is that you were true to your own essence.

Write your answer in your journal. Then take a deep breath, and remember how it feels to be true to yourself.

Prosperity Law #13
I Feel Good About Myself

Feeling good about yourself is priceless. We ultimately work through the prosperity process, or any life improvement process, to feel better about ourselves. Deep down, this is what we all desire.

Since the society we live in is externally focused, we are taught to look outward to feel good: to clothes, cars, jobs, houses, travel, relationships, etc. We believe these things will validate us and make us whole. But eventually we discover that looking outward does not guarantee happiness. When this realization occurs, the only solution remaining is to look for true fulfillment within ourselves.

The world within us is invisible, so at first it seems untouchable and unreachable. But since there is no outer answer, we find we must go more deeply inside. If we look within ourselves with honesty, we can sweep out the debris that keep us clogged with negativity, and replace them with a positive light.

Silently repeat the affirmation "I feel good about myself" for a minute or two, and reinforce it with thoughts and feelings about your positive qualities. Do this often, and lift yourself to a higher ground.

When you feel good about yourself,
the world becomes a more beautiful place.
You realize that you need nothing but the present moment
to be satisfied. Go within, and appreciate
the timeless essence that is you.

☞

Activity: *Feeling Good About Yourself*

Wherever you are right now, take a moment to relax and focus within. Sit or lie down comfortably, away from distractions. Close your eyes, and gently place your attention on your physical self. Just breathe, and be aware of your emotions and the sensations in and around your body.

Slowly take several deep breaths, and release tension each time you exhale. Remember to accept with love any emotions you may be experiencing. Allow yourself time to relax and loosen up. If you are very tense, this may take a few minutes.

When you feel peaceful, sense the spiritual essence that lies inside of you; become conscious of that part of you which simply notices and observes. This awareness within you is separate from your body. This is your infinite self.

In this and every moment, you are pure spirit, separate from the day-to-day foibles we all experience. Cast aside self-judgment, and stay mindfully aware of the loving energy that is your highest self. Take a moment to honor your infinite self and acknowledge your spiritual essence.

Remember this activity when you are tempted to be too critical of yourself. Know that this is the real you, and allow yourself to feel good about your *Self*.

Write about your experience in your journal.

Prosperity Law #14
I Easily Dissolve Limiting Beliefs and See Myself as I Really Am

If you could see the window of a baby's soul, it would be clear and shiny. The baby laughs with pure joy and cries with complete commitment. The baby knows what it wants, what it likes, and how it feels, and lets it show for all to see. Babies live in the moment with imagination, spontaneity, and confidence.

As children, most of us knew who we were and what we wanted to be when we grew up. Our thinking was limitless; we believed in magic and in our dreams. Nothing was impossible!

But as we grew older, we learned that we had to think and behave in certain ways to be acceptable. We began monitoring ourselves, acting mainly in ways that would garner the approval of others. Only as we "mature" do we forget our dreams and do only what we believe is practical and acceptable.

We need to shed any limiting thoughts and beliefs that are holding us back so that we can recreate the wondrous life that we knew was ours as children.

It is time to challenge old messages and belief systems. The thoughts you have that are limiting are a result of environmental conditioning. Let go of any ideas that keep you from being, doing, or having what you want.

Activity: *The Simple Things*

You don't have to fit into a specific mold to be a valuable person, and life doesn't have to be complicated to be worthwhile. Achievements have their place, but they do not measure your worth as a person. You are important simply because you are a part of this great universe.

Children don't question their abilities or self-worth. Unless they have been discouraged, they instinctively sense their immense potential. They are full of joy and wonder.

Think back to your childhood. Do your remember something that made you feel good and happy to be alive? Perhaps it was making up your own songs, smelling fresh cookies baking in the oven, looking forward to summer vacation, dancing joyfully for no reason, or simply lying in the grass.

Take a moment now to remember at least two simple pleasures from your childhood.

As you recall the simple things that triggered joy for you as a child, let these memories remind you of times when you automatically knew your intrinsic value as a being and sensed your unlimited potential. During these times you felt connected to your higher self and deserving of good simply because you were alive. Appreciate now that you, too, are one of the natural wonders of life.

Record your simple pleasures in your journal.

If you knew who walked beside you,

fear would be impossible.

—*A Course in Miracles*

5.

Partners in Time

To choose prosperity is to choose a spiritual path, as true prosperity is comprised of both material *and* nonmaterial wealth. This wealth includes riches such as love, self-expression, serenity, and a connection to your higher spiritual self, as well as financial prosperity.

True prosperity involves following your inner compass, discovering your purpose, and using your work to bring joy and peace into the lives of others.

When we live in fear and anxiety, all we can do is worry about ourselves: our problems, debts, resentments, and self criticisms. This is poverty thinking, and it doesn't leave any room for giving, gratitude, or charity. It is a very self-centered way of being. We end up living in competition with others, and it's every person for himself.

Becoming truly prosperous includes building a personal relationship with your higher power and looking towards your spiritual self to fulfill your needs.

When we realize that abundance is natural and when we allow our spiritual intelligence to lead us to a life of prosperity, we include others in our joy and our dreams, wanting to use our talents, riches, and fortune for the good of all.

Prosperity Law #15
I Am Aware of My Inner Being as the True Source of My Prosperity

Nature is inherently abundant and limitless. We can find myriad examples of extravagance in our universe; we have stars as far as the eye can see, and no one knows for sure what lies beyond. We can also break down physical form and find the same limitless qualities in atomic particles.

The invisible force that maintains this abundant universe also breathes life into every molecule of our bodies. This loving force is within and around all of us. It gives us life and sustains us. We each have a portion of this power and can use it as we wish.

When you become conscious of this energy and direct it with your intention, you will discover that you can apply it naturally to create harmony, abundance, and joy in your life.

Within each of us is a presence—
something that knows and notices. Be aware of this presence,
for it is what gives you life and sustains you.
Your prosperity does not depend on events in the outer world
but on your inner awareness of your consciousness
as the source of all your good.

Prepare to Meet Your Maker

Every culture in history has recognized a higher spiritual power, given it a name, and built certain rules and rituals around pleasing it. In today's societies, we have many different names, faces, and stories to describe it.

Unfortunately, due to the rigid traditions and religious practices with which many of us were raised, we were taught that this force is an angry, condemning, and judgmental being to be feared. As a result, many people no longer wish to believe in a higher creative power and have turned away from the very energy that sustains us.

The creative force has little to do with religion, dogma, or ritual. Humans created those practices to describe and relate to the energy of the universe in their own way and to help the limited human mind better understand this incredible and overwhelming mystery.

In truth, we distance ourselves from this higher spiritual energy somewhat when we try to define our experience of it with just words. Relating to this universal energy is more of a personal experience. We must each have our own relationship with it in order to truly understand it.

To try to grasp the difference between this spiritual force and religion, let us compare this creative energy to an ocean. This ocean is so vast and so powerful that human beings cannot fully comprehend its greatness. Yet all cultures sense that this mighty ocean is a vital part of their existence, so they strive toward a deeper understanding of it.

To this end, each culture captures a portion of the ocean in a test tube, to analyze and describe this great force. They place their tubes into the water and trap a few drops. The water in the tube is not the actual ocean, as it contains only a tiny part of it. Yet isolating the great body of water in this way is the only method they have to break down the ocean and attempt to fathom it more clearly.

While all cultures take water from the same ocean, the test tubes each culture uses to capture the ocean's essence are all different. Some tubes are small, some are large. Some are made of glass, some of plastic. Some are clean, some are dusty, some are muddy. Some tubes are cast deep into the ocean, while others are placed closer to the shore. The type, size, and placement of each tube colors the way the water is seen by the culture it belongs to, and yet the ocean itself is the same for all.

Just as the different tubes of water allow each culture to isolate and break down the ocean into more understandable proportions, religion allows us to break the vast creative intelligence down into more fathomable concepts for our particular culture. But ultimately, the water in the test tubes is not the ocean, just as religions are not the creative intelligence. Religion is a framework or filter with which we view and relate to the great energy that permeates our universe.

The test tubes cannot fully capture the mighty power of the ocean; similarly, religions cannot completely capture the full essence of the great creative force. As such, allowing religion alone to define our spiritual beliefs limits us. Religions are created by and for various groups of people through-out the centuries. Religion is a paradigm through which to relate to God. Yet ultimately, connecting with your higher spiritual power is a personal experience which lies within.

Activity: *Claiming and Naming Your Power*

In this prosperity program, we refer to the infinite intelligence mostly with words such as "creative force," "higher power," and, sometimes, "God." We do so because this seems to be the simplest way to name it. In reality, almost all words used to name this great force are inadequate, but we do the best we can within the confines of language.

Do not let these labels hinder you in developing your personal concept of a higher power. Refer to it in any way that feels comfortable to you. You can even consider it male, female, both, or neither; any age, race, or culture; animal, vegetable, or mineral; and all or none of the above. The important thing is to develop a concept that is personal and meaningful to you.

Find one or more names that you want to use to relate to the creative intelligence. Some people are comfortable with "God," and others are not. Many people today like to call it "higher power" or "great spirit." Maybe you don't want to use words and would rather relate to it more as a picture or a feeling or a sound. Select whatever names work best for you.

Record your names in your journal.

Prosperity Law #16
The Greatest of These Is Love

Most people sense that love is a great and almighty force. Love is the strongest bond between humans. We also feel love for other forms of life, such as our animal companions. We see powerful examples of love in the animal kingdom as well, a mother bear with her cubs, for instance.

Time and time again, people who report near-death experiences speak of meeting a loving, brilliant white light, and the only question they are asked is, "How have you expanded your ability to love?" Not, "How many hours did you put in at the office?" "How many home-runs did you hit?" or "How many widgets did you sell?" People on their deathbeds rarely wish they had spent more time in the office. They regret not having allowed themselves to express and experience more love.

Love can move mountains, love is expansive, and love is the way of the universe. When you carry love in your heart, life is easier and feels better. Love ultimately makes life worthwhile.

We are placed on this earth to learn how to truly love. God loves us and rewards us for loving with all forms of prosperity. Many say God is love. Every moment when you can choose between love and something else, choose love.

Love is the greatest force in the universe. Applying love to everything you do causes your path to unfold smoothly and draws your dreams in the perfect way. Expand your ability to love, and you will create magic and harmony in all your affairs.

I have never met a person whose greatest need

was anything other than real, unconditional love.

You can find it in a simple act of kindness

toward someone who needs help.

There is no mistaking love.

You feel it in your heart.

It is the common fiber of life,

the flame of that heats our soul,

energizes our spirit

and supplies passion to our lives.

It is our connection to God and to each other.

—Elizabeth Kubler-Ross

Activity: *Get to Know the Creative Intelligence*

Everything on this earth is made to sustain life. Each plant, insect, and animal has a purpose to maintain harmony and balance in the ecosystem, and we humans are no exception. We are also here to love, learn, and grow. But mostly we are here to learn to love.

Only an enlightened being or intelligence could have created this universe in all its infinite perfection. People often think of this being as judgmental and harsh, but by the law of the universe, an enlightened being could not have those qualities. Those negative energies vibrate at a low rate and are attached to the ego. Enlightenment means you have no ego.

Living a spiritual or enlightened life turns you into an incredibly powerful being. You become a person who emanates love, a person who does not judge, and a person who is filled with positive energy. That is the model of how to be like God.

All cultures agree that God is omnipotent. Most agree that God is love. If this is true, then God wants the best for you. God created you and is here for you.

With this new paradigm, describe seven or more positive qualities you want your higher spiritual power to have: compassionate, unconditionally loving, generous, wise, kind, understanding, maternal, paternal, and so on. The sky is the limit. Using the list below as an example, write your answers in your journal.

When you are finished writing, this list becomes your personal understanding of a higher power. Copy your answers onto a piece of paper or a 3 x 5 card, carry it with you, and refer to it often. Whenever you want to connect with the creative force, remember this list of attributes.

My Higher Power Is:

· *Loving*

· *Forgiving*

· *Compassionate*

· *Powerful*

· *Gentle*

· *Protective*

· *All-knowing*

Stay still, be quiet,

and listen to your heart.

Then when it speaks,

get up and go where it takes you.

—Susanna Tamaro

6.

Guidance

The creative intelligence is infinitely powerful and loving. That means we can rely on it to be here for us when feel we are alone. If we have problems that seem bigger than we are, we can ask our higher spiritual power for help. The answers are here if we are willing to listen.

You can communicate your needs as well as your gratitude to your higher power. You may have small requests or large requests. The only requirement is that you do not wish ill on anyone or act in ways that are harmful to others.

When you ask for guidance or anything else, know that the answers will come in the perfect way when the time is right. The creative intelligence has a perfect plan and cosmic timing. Even if you don't feel it right now, your higher power is still here. Just know this, and allow yourself to sense its presence within you.

Prosperity Law #17

I Connect with My Inner Power and Expand My Ability to Receive

Too many people erroneously believe that working harder will make them more prosperous. But working harder is not always the answer; you must work smarter.

The way to do this is first to become quiet and to become aware of your higher power. Release all fears and anxiety about your circumstances. Affirm prosperity, ask for guidance, and listen. Follow your intuition.

As you cultivate awareness of this creative energy, you will discover a loving force that directs and guides you towards prosperity.

As each individual is different, this program is designed to work for everyone, regardless of his or her spiritual or religious background. It is essential, however, that you believe that your life has a higher purpose and that the creative intelligence that sustains life in our universe works with you and through you, for the greater good of all.

Working harder is not necessarily going to bring
more prosperity to you. Abundance in your life depends
on your consciousness, not on a flurry of activity.
First you must go within and open your mind to receiving
great riches; then creating prosperity will be joyful and easy.

Activity: *Connecting to Your Higher Spiritual Power*

Find a quiet place where you will not be disturbed. Sit with your spine straight and your palms face up on your lap. Take several deep breaths, and allow any tension in your muscles to drain out of your body.

When you are comfortable, use the following breathing exercise to help you calm your mind and body: inhale slowly for ten counts. Hold this breath for four counts; then exhale slowly for ten counts. When you have released all your breath, pause for four counts; then begin to inhale again slowly for ten counts and repeat the cycle a few more times. Give yourself the time to relax.

Once you are feeling an inner sense of peace, place your attention in your heart area, and slowly become aware of an unconditionally loving energy that resides there. Imagine strong loving arms cradling you and infusing your entire being with comfort and love.

Visualize your heart radiating like a brilliant sun. Breathe deeply and steadily, and feel this loving and compassionate energy spread through your body.

As the feeling of love expands throughout your body, know that you are worthy of all the love and joy of the universe. The universe will give you what you want and need if you can allow yourself to accept it, so let it in. Understand that the divine intelligence always has the best for you in mind.

Know that this divine intelligence will guide you to greater abundance and prosperity. Give thanks for the perfect outcome that is to be realized.

Record your experiences in your journal.

Prosperity Law #18

I Trust That My Inner Guidance Will Lead Me to My Dreams

You have been granted this gift of life, this great miracle. The intelligence that created you intends for you to thrive. If you let your higher power guide you, the fruits of your efforts will be a thousand fold.

Sit quietly each day, and ask for guidance. Develop a trusting relationship with your higher spiritual power in which you learn to listen to and rely on your inner guidance. Your intuition is like a magical compass. You don't need to *do* anything. Just learn to be open and receptive.

Let the answers be revealed to you.

This power, with its unfathomable wisdom and intelligence, has your greater good in mind. So even if you do not know exactly what you want to create, you can ask your higher power to work through you for the highest good of all concerned. When you ask for guidance and listen, miracles happen in your life.

Guidance often comes into your life
in the form of an idea or a "gut feeling."
Trust your hunches and intuitions;
they will lead you in the direction of your dreams.

Activity: *Listening to Your Inner Guidance*

As children, we are often told to deny our true feelings and to ignore our intuition. We are trained not to listen to our inner voice, and eventually we can no longer hear it speak.

Learn to hear it again.

Become aware of what your intuition is telling you. It will speak to you in many ways. Be open and receptive to your inner voice, and a trusting partnership will develop.

In your Prosperity Journal, write about a time when you had an intuition about something good that came to pass, or write about inner guidance you have received. You may want to start a section in your journal where you can keep a record of your intuitions that manifest themselves. Reviewing these incidences regularly will help you learn to trust your inner guidance even more.

The following exercise helps you actively employ your inner guidance:

Write down a question that you want an answer to, and place it in a special section in your home. This might be a place where you meditate or keep pictures and objects that have meaning to you. Light a candle in this special space, and ask your higher self for an answer. Affirm that the perfect answer will come to you when the time is right. Then, release the question and wait.

The response could appear in the form of a symbol, a dream, a comment from someone else, or a spontaneous thought in your mind. Stay open to the various possibilities, and be patient. When the reply comes, write both the question and the answer you received in your Prosperity Journal.

You need not leave your room.

Remain sitting at your table and listen.

You need not even listen, simply wait,

just learn to become quiet and still and solitary.

Your world will freely offer itself to you

to be unmasked. It has no choice;

it will roll in ecstasy at your feet.

—Franz Kafka

7.

Being Still

The mantra is an ancient tool used in meditation to quiet the mind and to increase awareness of your higher spiritual power. When you are free from the noise of the mind, the infinite creative force makes its presence known.

Mantras are sacred words or phrases that hold universal, divine vibrations. When combined with positive intent, these vibrations spark healing energies. Whether said aloud or internally, repeated mantras seep into your consciousness, transforming your state of being and your environment, and connect you to the greater consciousness.

You can use a mantra as an affirmation or as a comforting phrase when you are troubled or worried—sort of a "first-aid" treatment for the mind and soul. This brings you back to your natural state of stillness and inner peace.

Breathe deeply, and repeat the words of the mantra silently or out loud. Then focus inward and listen. You must surrender doubts and misgivings and step aside to allow prosperity to flow freely into your life.

Prosperity Law #19
Be Still, and Know That I Am God

This statement is a mystical affirmation from the Bible. It means that the way to connect with your higher power is through the stillness of your soul. Silence is how we come to know God intimately.

When we use the word *God*, we are referring to your personal understanding of a higher spiritual power. Remember, this power is a loving force that is always present, whether you are aware of it or not. Your understanding of this infinite energy will deepen and grow as you practice the prosperity principles and do the activities in this guide.

When you say "I AM," you are using two of the most powerful and creative words in our language. The words "I AM" permeate your being, and whatever words you say with feeling in a sentence thereafter become part of your very essence. When you repeat "Be still, and know that I am God," you are affirming that God is within you, around you, and a part of you, as you are a part of It.

Through the stillness, you have firsthand experience of your infinite inner power. No one need tell you how to define it or communicate with it. You sense its presence in a personal way.

Quieting the mind in daily meditation
helps develop your powers of concentration.
It will give you a light, fresh perspective
and help you to become aware of the infinite power
within you that is the source of all your good.

Quietude

Say the phrase *"Be still, and know that I am God"* during meditation or during any activity. This powerful affirmation helps you to touch the source of your being. You can repeat this sentence as you would a mantra and change the energy in and around you.

The following, an excerpt from Mark Fisher's book *The Instant Millionaire: A Tale of Wisdom and Wealth*, illustrates the power of this ancient declaration.

Tranquility is the Greatest Manifestation of Power

Repeat "Be still and know that I am God" every day as often as you can. It will bring you the serenity so necessary for getting through life's upheavals.

When my mentor decided to reveal it to me, he said that of all the secrets in the world, this one was the most precious. It was his spiritual legacy to me, as it is mine to you.

By repeating this formula, which seemed strange to me at first, I developed a new inner power. This power, which never ceased growing over the years, kept reminding me of something the old millionaire had repeated to me over and over again: I could do anything, nothing would be impossible for me as soon as I became the master of my destiny. So, little by little, I convinced myself that I could steer my life exactly where I wanted it to go.

The more often you repeat the formula "Be still and know that I am God," the more powerful your inner voice will become, and the more surely it will guide you. The stronger your mind becomes, the more you realize there's nothing it can't accomplish.

The Power of the Mantra

This process of becoming still and remembering God (or your higher spiritual power) brings healing forces to your aid. When you repeat affirmations or a mantra with sincerity and gratitude in your heart, you unleash energies that raise your consciousness to a new level.

All cultures have phrases or prayers that you can repeat as you would a mantra with powerful results. Say these or other words, chants, or songs that have meaning to you. Use them in times of trouble, or any time you wish. Then focus inwardly and listen.

The Irish chanted the Prayer of St. Patrick in wartime for protection and courage when they were greatly outnumbered. This prayer can be used to gather strength and inner-peace:

Christ be with me, Christ before me, Christ behind me,
Christ beside me, Christ beneath me, Christ above me,
Christ within me, Christ where I live, Christ where I sit,
Christ where I arise, Christ in all I meet.

Imagine a brilliant white light within and around you as you say this.

You may wish to research ancient cultures to discover the words they used as mantras, or you may want to use your own affirmation. Allow the mantra or affirmation to help conjure up feelings of confidence, inner strength, protection, and love.

Prayer is speaking to God.
Meditation is listening.

—Unknown

The Most Ancient Mantra

Many scientists today agree with the ancient idea that, at their most fundamental level, all things in existence are made up of vibrating, pulsing energy. The earth itself is known to vibrate at a rate of 8 Hz per second.

From this energy emanates what many believe to be the primordial sound of the universe, the sound "OM." Throughout the ages, mystics have reported hearing this humming vibration, which permeates all of creation. With our modern scientific instruments, we have evidence that this sound exists.

The sound OM (pronounced AH—OH—MM) is the most ancient mantra and has its roots in Vedism (the precursor to Hinduism). OM is the most sacred word for the Hindus because it represents all the names and concepts of God. Moreover, OM offers a direct connection with your divine inner self. People have used this mantra for thousands of years to calm and center the restless mind. When we are free from the unquiet mind, we are more receptive to experiencing the higher self and to hearing the still, small voice of truth that resides within us.

Chanting OM from the depth of your being elevates your consciousness and allows you to delve into the stillness of your soul. Slowly chant AH-OH-MM, focusing on the sound. After chanting for several minutes, when you feel whole or serene, allow yourself to become mindful of the silence beyond the sound.

The creative energy is within us, yet this energy is much greater than you or I alone. Everything that sustains us is part of this great force. And because this loving universal energy has a master plan, it is vital that we come to trust and work with it.

Activity: *Being Still*

In the stillness reside all your answers. Spend a few minutes each day sitting quietly, away from all distractions such as people, the radio, the television, or the telephone.

If you are a beginner, start sitting for five minutes. You may notice at first that your mind is chattering away and flitting from thought to thought. This is fine. Even a mere second spent in stillness can transform your day and your internal state of being. The important thing is to begin the practice; then you can increase the time, little by little.

Spend these moments quietly reflecting inward. At first you may wish to repeat to yourself a phrase such as "I am peaceful and calm," if this helps you to relax. Remember to breathe deeply.

When you feel sufficiently tranquil, begin to meditate upon the mantra "OM" or, if you prefer, "Be still, and know that I am God." Choose any phrase, mantra, or affirmation which resonates with you, or just focus on your breathing.

Allow yourself time to become submerged in the mantra; after a while, stop the repetition, and listen to your inner voice. What is it saying to you? You may hear silence; you may hear thoughts. Be with whatever comes up for you. Just observe, as a witness would.

By practicing this discipline daily, you connect with your soul and enhance all areas of your life. Try this activity now. *Journal your daily observations.*

Prosperity Law #20
I Go Within and Focus
on What I Want to Create

Rather than focusing so much attention on a problem, look to the solution. Too often we dwell upon what is wrong, failing to spend much time considering how to right it. Not only is this an unproductive habit; it also compounds the problem. Remember, *what you concentrate on expands*. Focus on the problem, and what you see (the problem) is what you get (more of the same problem).

You direct your energy with your thoughts, emotions, intentions, and awareness. When you notice that you are entertaining thoughts of fear, worry, or negativity, refocus your energy, and remind yourself that you attract prosperity with silent confidence.

Learn to trust the process of creation. The universe works in your favor when you honor and respect its laws. As your relationship with the creative intelligence grows, you will develop a serene sense of confidence that it takes care of you.

When a worry thought arises, use it as a signal to go within and focus on the new reality you are creating for yourself. Reclaim your personal power by releasing the worry thought and replacing it with a positive affirmation.
You create your circumstances
by the thoughts you repeatedly think.

Activity: *Focus on Prosperity*

What do you want to create? Right now, take a worry thought, and turn it into a positive affirmation that you can repeat to yourself. Write out this new affirmation as a positive statement; say it in the present tense and in first person.

For instance, instead of saying "I never have enough money," tell yourself, "I always have enough money, and I am well taken care of." *Feel* this statement as your reality *now*.

Let go of any negative images in your mind of what you fear may happen, and picture the situation working out exactly as you want it to. Remember to breathe deeply throughout this activity.

Instead of focusing on the situation you want to avoid or get rid of, concentrate on allowing your new desired reality to manifest. Be tenacious and persistent about saying the affirmation to yourself and feeling it as truth. Patiently allow for the *time* to turn things around.

Do this on a regular basis. Keep the positive image in mind, and be patient. Do not let yourself fixate on what you do not want to happen. This does not help anyone. Focus on what you want.

These simple exercises applied in conjunction with the other activities in this book will help you develop a new outlook, raise your energy, and create wonderful new results in your life. *Record your observations and experiences in your journal.*

If you want to experience prosperity

at a miraculous level,

you must leave behind your old ways of thinking

and develop a new way

of imagining what is possible for you

to experience in your life.

—Dr. Wayne Dyer

8.

Becoming a Prosperity Thinker

You can count how many seeds are in an apple,
but no one knows for sure
how many apples are in a seed.
—Unknown

Your thoughts have the power to transform your life. Tend to them carefully and lovingly as though you were tending to a beautiful garden. The mental and emotional energies you send out constantly impress the universal mind. The universe responds by putting into your life that which you are *being* in mind, emotion, and spirit. Prosperity thinking is essential if you want to be prosperous, because *you are what you think about all day long.*

Most people try to apply the prosperity principles in the wrong order. They think that they need to *have* things so that they can *do* what they want and *be* who they want to be. But the opposite is true. You need to first *be* who and what you want to be in mind and spirit; then you will *do* the things that kind of a person would do, and as a result, you will *have* what you want in your life. Abundance comes naturally when you are thinking and acting with prosperity consciousness.

Give joyfully of that which you seek. You will find that life always gives back more in return. Some things, such as love, aren't really even yours until you give them away. So give as if they are in infinite supply, because they are.

Prosperity Law #21
I Am Ready and Willing to Change

We say we want change, but we are not always prepared for what that means. Often, we are more invested than we realize in keeping things the same. At times we must give up comfort temporarily in order to adjust to a different life or lifestyle. This can make real change more difficult than we had originally anticipated.

Learning the Universal Laws of Prosperity is like taking a magic shortcut. You are consciously letting go of struggle and worn-out ways of doing things that hold you back. The Universal Laws will help you go through the transformation process more smoothly.

An inner shift is often necessary before we are truly ready to take in a new way of being. As you repeat to yourself "I am ready and willing to change," you will sense a change inside you. This affirmation will help you knock down inner walls that are blocking your growth. Say this phrase to yourself often, especially when you have a new vision of something that you want to create in your life.

In following your new path of prosperity,
be ready to do things in a completely different way
than you are accustomed. Open yourself to change,
and the road will unfold with many pleasant surprises.
Prepare to experience life in a new way.

Activity: *Willingness*

Pause for a moment, and take a deep breath. Close your eyes and say to yourself, "I am ready and willing to change." Repeat this affirmation several times. Notice what you feel inside—how willing are you really? Are you struggling to hold onto old unproductive habits?

If you sense you are not willing to change but would like to be, say to yourself, "I am willing *to be willing* to change."

Allow yourself to relax, let go, and open up to change. Repeat this affirmation when you want to create change easily, or use it the next time you feel resistant to making a positive change in your life.

Record your observations in your journal.

Prosperity Law #22
I Have an Attitude of Gratitude

Gratitude in Webster's dictionary is defined as "thankful appreciation for favors received." How many of us think of our belongings, good experiences, friendships, and other valuables as *favors received?* We often pay little or no attention to our daily blessings and focus instead on what is still missing in our lives. Become aware of the wonderful things already in your life. Everything you now have *is* a favor received.

Gratitude paves the way for more beauty to come into your life. There is a saying in the Bible: *To those who have, more will be given. To those who have not, even what little they have will be taken away.* In other words, when you are thankful for what you *have*, however great or small, your life will seem full, and you will attract even more prosperity as a result.

However, if you focus on poverty or on what you *don't* have, you will repel good things from your life, and you will not even notice or appreciate the prosperity that you already have.

Meister Eckhart, a 13th century philosopher, said, "If the only prayer you ever say is 'thank you' it will be enough." Actively saying "thank you" to the universe fills you with the energies of love and gratitude and gives you an overwhelming sense of natural abundance.

> *Thankfulness is a deep appreciation*
> *for everything you have in your life.*
> *Approach life with an attitude of gratitude,*
> *and you will enjoy all you now have,*
> *and all that is to come.*

Activity: *Building Your Attitude of Gratitude*

Realize that your life is already full of riches. We live on a planet surrounded by art in motion. We have an abundance of food to eat, water to drink, and air to breathe. We enjoy seemingly ordinary wealth such as good health, friendships, and good luck.

We can experience more abundance by being thankful for the wealth we possess *now*. When you have an idle moment, count your blessings. Doing so at bedtime, at meals, and upon waking is a wonderful way to attract prosperity. Do this every day, and your abundance will grow. Remember: to those who have, more will be given.

Study the sample gratitude list below, and then write in your journal your own list of at least seven things for which you are thankful.

I Am Grateful for:

1. Serenity.

2. My musical talent.

3. The joy of watching my dog play.

4. Good health for myself, my friends, and my family.

5. Synchronicities or miracles.

6. Unexpected income.

7. Feeling guided and watched over by my higher power.

Prosperity Law #23
I Am Prosperous in All Areas of My Life

All of which we behold is full of blessings.
—William Wordsworth

Practice prosperity thinking daily, as you would practice any new skill. Negative habits can be deeply ingrained, and you may not recognize how much energy you are generating to keep them locked in place. Become aware of the time you spend thinking negatively, and make a conscious decision to recycle that same energy through a positive funnel instead.

The tendency to focus on what is lacking is not necessarily a personality flaw but a naturally inherited trait that enables us to take care of ourselves by making us aware of our needs. It does little to attract prosperity to us, however, and breaking this pattern is necessary if we wish to create a prosperous life.

Instead of focusing on what you feel you don't have, notice the abundance all around you. Look at life with the eyes of a prosperous person. See the glass of water as half-full rather than half-empty. Pay regular attention to cultivating your new prosperity habits and lifestyle.

One way you can do this is to talk to yourself about all the things you have in your life that you appreciate. Actively remind yourself about all the beauty that surrounds you now.

Wonderful things are in your life right now.
Practice noticing them.
When you turn your thoughts to the abundance
you already have, you dissolve scarcity
and draw more good into your life.
Remind yourself daily of your blessings.

Activity: *The Prosperity Circle*

The prosperity circle is a great way to visualize the prosperity that is around you now, as well as the prosperity coming to you. The general perception is that we move toward events in a linear fashion. But it can be helpful to look at life in a more circular way. Try seeing yourself as the center of your universe and thinking of events in your life as *moving toward you.*

The prosperity circle illustrates the types of prosperity that your thoughts and energies are manifesting and attracting. Create your prosperity circle by first writing your name in the center of a page in your journal and then drawing several circles around it, each one larger than the next. Draw the outermost circle with dashes or dots.

In the solid circle, list four or more types of prosperity presently surrounding you. This part of the diagram illustrates the prosperous energy that is expressing itself in your life now.

In the outer dotted circle, list four or more types of prosperity that your thoughts are pulling toward you right now. This part of the diagram illustrates the prosperity that is in the process of moving into your life.

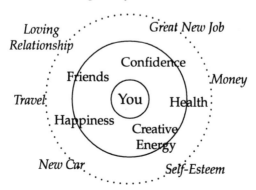

Nurture the thoughts and energies you want to manifest.

Prosperity Law #24
I Am Generous with Myself and Others

When I was six or seven years old, growing up
in Pittsburgh, I used to take a precious penny of my own
and hide it for someone else to find.
—Annie Dillard

To give is divine. To receive is also divine. In the broadest sense, giving and receiving are both the same—merely different aspects of the eternal flow. Giving and receiving with regularity keep a natural ebb and flow in motion in your life.

When you give to others, you discover the deep satisfaction of giving. Giving with love is the highest form of generosity and creates joy and space in your life from which to receive.

Receiving with love allows others the opportunity to experience the joy of giving. Remember also to be generous with yourself.

Let go of possessions lightly. Nothing is really ours; we are only borrowing things for a short time. Holding on tightly clogs the system. We must each discover our own personal rhythm of giving and receiving. Balance is the key.

You must be able to give in order to receive.
What you get back will be tenfold.
Don't hold tightly to your possessions.
Always give with a light heart and the knowledge that
more abundance is waiting to flow into your life.

Activity: *Generosity Meditation*

I give gladly with love,

I expect nothing in return.

I receive with gratitude

and feel deserving and worthy.

The prosperity of the universe

flows through me.

My life is full of love and abundance.

I always have more than enough.

There are human societies so simple and unadorned

as to possess no clothing other than the loincloth,

no tool other than the stick or stone,

no permanent dwelling place,

no carving or plastic art.

But nowhere on this planet

can you find people without music or dance.

—George Leonard

9.

The Pulse of Life

We must accept that this creative pulse within us
is God's creative pulse itself.
—Joseph Chilton Pearce

The universe is energy, and energy consists of repeating rhythms and vibrations. There is a constant ebb and flow to all living things, and a silent steady pulse. This is the rhythm of life.

Getting in tune with this pulse transforms your experience of living. When you join this flow, everything seems to go your way, and you are in harmony with life. You feel connected to your higher power, and prosperity becomes natural.

Think about the repeated rhythms happening around you. Take in all the possible cycles or rhythms you can: the flapping of a bird's wings; the cycles of the seasons; the repeated rhythms in a musical composition; the sound of footsteps. All these rhythms sustain life on our planet.

Consider how the rhythm of life also operates in the world of our finances. Money comes in from revenues or a job and goes out for expenses. At alternate times in a financial cycle, we see surpluses and deficits. This money cycle is as true for individuals and small businesses as it is for large corporations. Money has a rhythm and flow, just like everything else.

Prosperity Law #25
I Live in the Flow and the Rhythm of Life

We each have a rhythm that is uniquely our own, yet it connects us to everything in the universe. When we learn to align our personal rhythm with the pulse of the universe, we tune in to the endless and perfect flow.

Think of your breath. You started breathing from the moment you were born. And before you were born, your heart was pumping blood back and forth through your veins and arteries.

Consider the oceans. On beaches all around the world, the tides flow continually in and out. At the same time, jet streams blow weather systems perpetually across the globe. And as the sun tirelessly dawns and sets somewhere in the world, the earth's surface constantly moves and changes.

As you practice being with your personal rhythms, you will find yourself synchronizing with the universal energy. When you are in the flow, the details of your life will seem to fall into place effortlessly.

All aspects of your life, including prosperity, have a natural cycle. The prosperity tide in your life goes out, then comes back in—goes out, and comes in again. Be conscious of this constant ebb and flow. Awareness of your own prosperity cycle or pulse puts you in the easy flow of giving and receiving.

Experience the rhythms of life, and
stay aware of the prosperity cycles of ebb and flow.
We are ultimately made of energy, and we attract that which
resonates with our own rhythm. Trust that when the flow of
prosperity goes out, it will always come back in.

Activity: *Experiencing the Pulse of Life*

Sit or lie down in a quiet place, and relax. Listen to your breathing. Feel your heartbeat. Become intimately aware of the unending pulsation of energy throughout your body. Stay with these rhythms for several minutes.

When you are ready, expand your awareness to some of the rhythms that surround you right now: the ticking of a clock, the humming of a refrigerator, the whirring motor of a passing car, the gentle tapping of rain, the rushing sound of the wind. Then on a larger scale, become aware of the orbits of the moon around the earth, the earth around the sun, and our solar system in the galaxy.

Every living being on this planet has a pulse (repeated rhythms) and internal cycles that keep it alive. Stay aware of your inner-rhythm, and connect it with the pulsation of rhythm you hear, feel, and sense around you.

Coexist in this symphony of rhythm, within and without, and allow a feeling of connectedness with the pulse of the universe to grow and expand. With the heightened awareness of this intimate connection you have with all of life, you will sense yourself to be a part of the eternal dance of energy.

Keep cultivating this experience. Don't worry if it takes time to develop fully; simply persist and be consistent in your practices. Do this exercise each day for a few minutes to experience your alignment with the rhythms of life. As you become more in tune with the rhythm of the universe, more prosperity will flow to you, and things will naturally work out in your favor.

Record your daily observations in your journal.

The goal should not be to make money

or acquire things

but to achieve the consciousness

through which the substance will flow forth

when and as you need it.

—Eric Butterworth

10.

Money and You

Money is a difficult topic for most people to talk about. Much of our self-image and self-worth is built around what we have (or don't have). Many people would rather discuss anything than the state of their finances.

In *Secrets to Lifelong Prosperity*, we distinguish between two realms of money. The first is the inner realm: how we feel about and relate to the collective issues of money, abundance, and prosperity. The second is the outer realm: how our money functions in the world.

The outer realm, dealing with the way money is best handled, saved, and invested, is a separate topic, sometimes changing from year to year. This outer realm of money has its own set of rules and guidelines. Many timely books and articles are available on this topic.

Suze Orman has an excellent system for managing money which dovetails nicely with our prosperity program. If you are interested in learning more about money management, you may wish to read her books, or visit her Web site at http://www.SuzeOrman.com

In *Secrets to Lifelong Prosperity*, we are studying the inner realm of money, including the effects of our thoughts, beliefs, and emotions on our prosperity and money, and the rules that never change: *The Universal Laws of Prosperity*.

Modern Money Myths

From the time we are young, many of us hear that money is the root of all evil; money can't buy happiness; rich people are bad and may not get into heaven. These attitudes are so firmly entrenched in our minds that we are often not aware of them. Is it any wonder that many people believe that money is dirty, or evil?

The belief that money is bad is based in part on a passage in the Bible, which states, "The love of money is the root of all evil." In this sentence, money itself is not the root of all evil, but the importance we place on money in our lives is. The phrase "the love of money" connotes making money your god and putting its importance above all else.

Money itself is not bad or evil. Money is just a unit of exchange. Evil comes about when people, believing in scarcity or seeking power, place the value of money over the value of life. Money itself is neutral. "Good" or "evil" comes from our actions and attitudes about money, and the way we treat others and our universe as a result.

People who believe in scarcity often destroy the earth and its natural resources or feel they must lie, cheat, or even kill for money. They cut down rain forests and ravage the earth, suppress entire nations, rig elections, create wars, hunt endangered animals, and promote and sell products that are unhealthful or even fatal to consumers and to our environment. Rather than believing in the idea that prosperity is available for all, they think it is "everyone for himself." This scarcity thinking only pushes prosperity away. We desperately need to check our attitudes and think in terms of abundance and balance instead of lack or chaos.

Money is a powerful tool in our society, a tool that we can use to help create a more positive world. So for our purposes, money will be used as a *symbol of energy*. This symbol will help us incorporate our higher vision into our daily lives and contribute to healing our planet.

Money may not buy happiness, but most of us need money to function smoothly in society. Those who do not have enough money to meet their needs often feel anxious and pressured to pay their bills. They feel they cannot relax and enjoy life because they need to run around trying to create more money. They feel limited in the positive experiences they can create and in the quality time they can spend with loved ones.

When you have a strong prosperity consciousness, you trust that the universe always provides for you, and you feel confident that there is always more than enough. You can follow your life's dreams and express your highest self. You can enrich the lives of others with your wonderful accomplishments. And you can gladly share your abundance by donating your time, money, or energy to causes you believe in, helping to make positive changes on a local and global basis.

Prosperity Law #26
I Give Back to the Universe
and Contribute to the Infinite Flow

Traditionally, tithing is known as giving a percentage of your income (usually ten percent) to the group, organization, or other source through which you experience your spiritual growth.

Tithing is a powerful action that demonstrates your faith in your higher power as the true provider of your prosperity. If the tithe is given freely, without ulterior motives, you experience a feeling of freedom and abundance, and your faith in the universal laws grows stronger than ever. Many of the most successful business people attribute their great prosperity to a regular practice of tithing.

If you are uncomfortable with giving ten percent, you can start by giving two or five percent, or whatever makes you feel comfortable. The important thing is to begin.

The prosperity law of tithing is based on the laws of nature. When a farmer reaps the harvest, one tenth is put back to nourish the soil. This is the infinite flow and circulation, and we become a part of it by both taking and giving.

Tithing is a way to return to the Universe
a percentage of your income for recirculation.
Balance your receiving by giving freely.
Giving opens the path for more prosperity to come
into your life and acknowledges your higher power
as the Source of all your good.

Activity: *The Practice of Tithing*

· Have you ever tithed?

· How do you feel about tithing?

· What are your fears about taking up the practice of tithing?

· What are the benefits you can see in choosing to tithe?

· Can you see how tithing relates directly to your sense of prosperity and how it actively demonstrates your faith in your higher power as the source of your abundance?

· Is there a group, organization, or other source that you would consider to be the wellspring of your spiritual food?

· If not, does an organization exist that cultivates the growth of your personal spiritual beliefs?

· If you were to tithe, what percentage of your income would you be comfortable giving?

· Are you willing to try this form of prosperity consciousness? If not, why not?

Ask yourself these questions, and write the answers in your journal.

Prosperity Law #27

I Have the Power to Create All the Money I Need

Abundance is the way of the universe. When you work with the creative force, you have access to more abundance than you may initially realize.

People who are constantly worried about making or losing money are not prosperous, no matter how financially successful they may be. Even Howard Hughes, one of the richest men in history, used to feel poor and worry about money.

Worrying about money leaves us feeling incapable of creating real financial security. Fear robs us of joy and keeps us closed to potential answers.

Money comes to you through a variety of channels, but the ultimate source of your money is your higher spiritual power. Feel gratitude for all the channels through which you receive your money, but always acknowledge that it comes from the one true source: the infinite universal intelligence—that which created everything in the first place. Open your mind up to abundance, and know that it is naturally right for you to prosper in all ways.

It is important to let go of any fears you have
about money or bills. When you worry about your bills,
you give away your power.
Trust that you have within you the power
to create all the money you could ever want or need.

Activity: *Personal Power*

This simple exercise helps to bring you into conscious contact with your inner power. Whenever you begin to worry about money, do not entertain thoughts of scarcity; instead, go to work on your consciousness right away. Think of the feeling of fear as a signal, and use it as an opportunity to rediscover your true power.

Close your eyes, and take a few deep and relaxing breaths through your nose; then exhale through your mouth, releasing any tension in your body with the air. As you breathe, feel the energy of the life force entering your body. Imagine your breath to be a brilliant white light that flows through you.

Consider the fact that there is an abundance of air for you to breathe, just as there is an abundance of most everything on our planet. Gently and confidently allow this abundant energy into your life and release any fears of scarcity you may have.

Silently thank the creative intelligence for all that you have now, and say to yourself, "God is the source of my prosperity."

Next, focus on your power center for a few minutes (your solar plexus, in the middle of your torso). Imagine a bright yellow ball of light glowing in your power center, and allow an inner strength and energy to build. Allow this ball of light to grow and surround you; then let it expand like a supernova out into the universe. Repeat to yourself the affirmation "I have the power to create all the money I need."

Take your time with this activity. Breathe the energy in and out, and allow your confidence to grow.

Record your experience in your journal.

Wealth is attracted to the person

who is emotionally and intellectually ready

to accept it, expect it, and enjoy it.

—*Jerry Gillies*

Prosperity Law #28
I Am Ready to Accept Wealth

We equate change with the unknown, and the unknown is often scary. Believe it or not, we often keep prosperity away because we are afraid of change; without realizing it, we may be putting out energy to keep things in our lives the same. This emotional block can be overcome by repeating:

I Am Ready to Accept Wealth.

Being ready to accept wealth as part of your transformation opens the channels to prosperity. By using this affirmation, you are trying on the feeling of prosperity and allowing yourself to accept it.

By wealth, we mean all the forms of prosperity that you can think of: health, well being, relationships, career, happiness, money, and so on. Practice mentally and emotionally accepting all forms of wealth into your life.

You may be blocking your riches
by unconsciously fearing change.
Confidently imagine that you are now prosperous,
and affirm that you are ready to accept abundance.
Open yourself mentally and emotionally to wealth.

Activity: *Accepting Wealth*

Throughout the day, repeat the affirmation *"I Am Ready to Accept Wealth."* This positive statement helps raise your energy and draws prosperity to you.

If you experience any persistent negative thoughts while saying this affirmation to yourself, write them on a piece of paper that is separate from your Prosperity Journal. We will discuss how to transform hindering thoughts into positive statements in an upcoming chapter.

Continue to ponder the affirmation *"I am ready to accept wealth,"* and practice letting it in. Think about and visualize the various forms of wealth you are attracting and allowing into your life. Imagine yourself in detail enjoying an abundance of prosperity, health, loving relationships, self-esteem, happiness, inner peace, and financial and career success.

Notice what each form of prosperity feels like, and how prosperity feels to you as a whole. Breathe deeply and accept more abundance each time you take a breath. Breathe out negativity, self-doubt, and fear of change. Breathe in prosperity, confidence, and tranquility.

By living your prosperity in this present moment, you become a powerful magnet for wealth and abundance.

Use your Prosperity Journal to record positive observations that result from saying this affirmation.

Prosperity Law #29
I Deserve Money

Many of us suffer from an inadequate self-image due to the negative messages we received as young children. Now, as adults, we may resist the idea of financial prosperity because of underlying feelings of low self-worth. These self-esteem issues are deeply ingrained and are sometimes so subtle that they are hard to see.

If you feel undeserving, you will push money or other forms of prosperity away, either by under-earning, over-spending, or finding some other tactic that keeps you from enjoying abundance.

If you want to know what your thoughts are regarding money, look to your environment for clues. The condition of your finances at this time indicates what you have believed and felt about money up until now.

As you work through negative thoughts and beliefs, be patient, and allow time for change to occur. Put a priority on loving yourself. As you improve your self-image and expand your feelings of self-worth, you will allow more money—as well as all the other forms of abundance—into your life.

We were not created to struggle. We were created to soar. We must recognize our divine nature and accept the abundance that is rightfully ours.

Realize that you do deserve to have money.
You deserve to have what you need and to feel secure.
Feeling deserving creates an opening in your life
through which to receive.

People will pay you money to a great extent

based on what value you place on yourself.

—*Jack Boland*

Activity: *Discovering Your Worth*

Use a separate piece of paper for this activity, not your journal.

Repeat to yourself the words "I deserve prosperity," and see what comes to mind. Do you feel completely in tune with this statement, or do you notice any resistance in your thoughts or feelings?

Now say "I deserve money," and notice your reaction. If any negative thoughts surface when you say either affirmation, write them out on a loose piece of paper. Repeat the affirmation a few more times, taking note of what comes forward. Most of us are not used to actively listening to what our subconscious has to tell us. It is important not to self-censor. Write down the thoughts as they come to you, even if they don't seem to make sense now.

When no more negative thoughts arise when you say this affirmation, read what you wrote down. If you think you are keeping money away from yourself, you can look at this list and understand why.

Now, write a positive affirmation in response to each negative thought. Write these affirmations in your Prosperity Journal. *When you are finished, keep the pages of negative thoughts; we will use them for an activity in Chapter 23, Releasing Negativity.*

Now that you have acknowledged those negative thoughts, write "I deserve money" in your journal, and focus on this as truth. Let the positive energy of this thought build inside of you; then adopt and integrate that energy into your consciousness by breathing deeply and fully accepting that you *are* deserving. As you perform these activities, you are transforming your energy. Your outer conditions will change as you adopt a new point of view. *Try this exercise with any affirmation you wish.*

Prosperity Law #30
I Am Debt Free

*It is important to realize that it is not really for lack of
abundance that you are experiencing want, but for lack of
awareness of the ever-present reality of divine substance, and
the faith to shape it into manifest form.—Eric Butterworth*

Telling yourself that you are debt-free can be difficult to do
when you've been worrying about your bills. The purpose of
such an affirmation is to get you to start thinking about
prosperity instead of debt. You can use the energy you are
wasting on worrying more constructively: by focusing on
what you want—rather than on what you don't want.

Prosperity is a way of *be-ing*. Gently teach yourself to feel
abundant, and you will find ways to allow more prosperity
to come into your life. As prosperity increasingly enters your
life, you will feel even more abundant.

If you have spent a lot of your energy focusing on debt,
you might not realize how invested you are in having to worry
about your finances. At first, it may feel strange to let go of
worrying. But we will fill the empty spot by replacing it with
more productive thoughts.

You may notice resistance to the affirmation "I am debt
free," because of all the time you have spent in the past
worrying. Try saying it during or after a good workout or
walk to expend your energies and lower your resistance to
letting go of debt and worry.

*Forgive yourself for incurring debt; then focus on your
incoming wealth. Let go of any negative feelings you have
about debt. Practice feeling your debts dissolve,
and send them away with love.*

Activity: *Letting Go of Bills*

Think of some bills you've been worrying about. Itemize them on a piece of paper with their significant details, including the amounts owed.

Now sit back in a comfortable position, and close your eyes. Breathe out any feelings of anxiety, and breathe in relaxation. Breathe out negativity and debt, and breathe in prosperity and abundance.

Practice saying "I am debt *free*. I am free." Focus on feeling free. Breathe in deeply, and let go of tension and worry when you let the breath out. Allow yourself to relax. Forgive yourself, and let go of any blame over the creation of the debt. Continue to do this even if you feel resistant.

Next, see yourself writing checks and sending them to your creditors stamped in red with the words, "Paid in full." Imagine all balances owed as $0.00. Send the checks off with love, and feel yourself becoming free.

The upward cycle begins by letting go of poverty consciousness and allowing yourself to feel, and to be, prosperous in the moment. Try to do this as long as you can, even if it is only for half a minute at first. For at least that thirty seconds, cast away all doubt, and hold vividly to your vision of prosperity.

Even this small amount of time can create a shift within you—and within the creative intelligence. With practice you will be able to visualize being debt free a little bit longer each time, and you will see positive changes occur in your world.

On a regular basis imagine your bills as Paid in Full. Write your experiences of this activity in your Prosperity Journal.

Prosperity Law #31
I Already Have the Money

The absolute truth is, there is no lack anywhere,
but and overflowing abundance of every kind of good
which you can possibly desire or conceive of.
—H. Emily Cady

The energy that you are generating is either attracting or repelling prosperity. Fear of scarcity works against you; fear tends to attract the situation you are trying to avoid. Strong inner confidence, on the other hand, draws money to you.

When we affirm and visualize something with feeling, we create an energy within and around us which helps to bring the desired situation about. Instead of worrying about our supply, we must confidently tell ourselves that the universe is taking care of us.

Your inner vision is powerful. If you can imagine it, then that situation is possible for you, and you can make the desired condition true for you. When you can cast away all doubt, you become a money magnet.

Remember that a force greater than you sustains our universe, and this force responds to the energy you are putting out now. Confidently affirm: "I already have the money." Then, give thanks in advance, knowing that you already have what you want.

You attract prosperity into your life with serene assurance.
Affirming that you already have the money
you desire is powerful. Give thanks in advance,
and confidently visualize your bills
as already paid in full.

Activity: *Abundance Meditation*

I know the true source of prosperity

is within me and all around me.

I am like a fish surrounded by the abundant

universal ocean.

I ask for sustenance and I shall receive.

I give thanks for my good,

and I give of myself.

The right things are here when I need them.

The universe rushes in to fill my life

with love and prosperity.

Prosperity Law #32
Problems Are Only Temporary

When you change the way you look at things,
the things you look at change.
—*Wayne Dyer*

Many people have a habit of complaining about anything that seems to be going wrong in the moment. They spend all their emotional energy focusing on what is lacking in their lives. By doing this, they give their power away.

You must keep your precious life energy for what you want to expand in your life—namely, the good. When you learn to focus on the good in your life, you sail through life more smoothly.

Most of what we consider to be problems are just daily annoyances. If you feel annoyed or anxious, ask yourself, "Will any of this really matter in one year?" Often, it won't even matter in twenty-four hours.

Bigger challenges are not necessarily all bad; they often turn out to be learning experiences that strengthen our character. There is a saying: "That which does not kill me makes me stronger." Once we have triumphed over our challenges, we can see that we are greater for having had those experiences. Approach both petty annoyances and greater challenges with an inner resolve that no matter how the situation looks on the surface, everything under the sun is here for your ultimate benefit and higher good.

Rise above the clouds, and you will see the sun.
In every problem lies opportunity; you need only look for it.
Still your mind, and you will be guided
to turn each challenge into a gift of growth.

Activity: *Practicing the Presence of God*

Emmet Fox, a great teacher and visionary, taught a clearing activity he called "The Golden Key." When you have a problem, he says to "Golden Key it." This means that when you are having a tough time, you can remember all the qualities of God. For instance, God is abundant, omnipotent, forgiving, omnipresent, all-knowing, unconditionally loving, caring, compassionate. Fox instructs us to, "Stop thinking about the difficulty, whatever it is, and think about God instead....If you are persistent enough, you will overcome any problem."

Remember all the qualities of God until you are so absorbed in these thoughts that you have put out of your mind, for a few moments at least, what is troubling you. Think about the list of traits you created on page 87 for your higher power.

This Golden Key activity charges your situation with new energy. It acknowledges that God is the source of all your good and strength, and it helps to dissolve the difficulty you are experiencing back into the nothingness from which it came.

"The Golden Key to harmony is in your hand now. It is God who works, and not you. Your particular limitations or weaknesses are of no account in the process. Your treatment will really be just the getting of yourself out of the way. All that is absolutely essential is to have an open mind, and sufficient faith to try the experiment."

You can do this activity several times a day if you wish, but let go of thinking about the situation between "Golden Key" sessions. And don't try to figure out how the problem will work itself out—that will only get in the way. Leave it up to God.

Try this activity now with a challenge you are facing in the present. When you are finished, surrender the challenge to the universe to be resolved, and repeat a positive affirmation.

Prosperity Law #33
I Love and Accept Myself

*Love yourself! Do it now! Don't wait until you get well
or lose the weight, or get the new job or the new relationship.
Begin now—and do the best you can.*
—Louise L. Hay

Wherever you are in your prosperity process is just fine. Remembering to love and accept yourself at whatever stage you are in at this time is vital to your growth. Until you can accept where you are right now, you will experience difficulty moving forward.

The reason for this is simple. If you are invested in feeling unacceptable, you will stay stuck. All the good energy you could be putting forth into growth is spent on criticizing yourself instead. Focusing on the negative only causes the negative to grow stronger and become more prominent in your life.

Once you choose to accept yourself fully, you will move more quickly and easily to where you want to be. Learn to accept yourself and your situation. Tell yourself that everything is all right and that problems are only temporary. Focus on appreciating your life and on being grateful for your positive qualities. From this position, you will loosen your grip on the old way of being and free your energy to move forward.

*There is no substitute for self-love and self-acceptance.
The more you love yourself, the more riches you will accept
into your life. Outer actions will be futile unless you
love yourself enough to receive your blessings.*

Activity: *Loving Yourself*

So how do we love and accept ourselves? This may seem like a tall order, since we may have spent most of our lives criticizing ourselves and believing the criticism of others.

We have already learned that criticism keeps us stuck. Therefore, the first step to loving yourself is to *stop all self-criticism*. We must *resolutely refuse* to criticize ourselves any longer. Constant criticism changes nothing. It only holds us back from growing, makes us feel bad, depletes our power, and wastes our energy.

When you notice that you are putting yourself down or saying something negative to yourself, just say to yourself, *"Stop!"* Stop those thoughts, and absolutely, positively refuse to criticize yourself any more. Replace the negative thoughts with the affirmation "I love and accept myself" or any other positive statement that builds you up.

Louis Hay, author of *You Can Heal Your Life*, suggests that when you see yourself in the mirror, look in your own eyes and say, "I love you, I really love you." Do this at least once a day.

If these activities sound self-indulgent to you, think of your options. You could just feel bad about yourself and be so self-absorbed that you have no space for anyone else in your heart. Or you could take all the negative energy that criticism creates and let it out on the people around you and stay miserable.

In the end, the more love you have for yourself, the more love you will have for others, and the more of a positive effect you will have on the world. So keep telling yourself that you love and accept yourself (despite your imperfections). Perform this exercise regularly. This activity can make a world of difference. *Record your observations in your Prosperity Journal.*

Let the river of your life flow freely and deeply,

and let the pebbles of your love fall into the water

to create ripples that will touch us all.

—Bernie Siegel, M.D.

11.

Harmony with Others

Life's journey is always easier
when you hear a friend's footsteps beside you.

—Unknown

We all are part of the same great power and have been given special talents that are unique to each of us. A person with prosperity consciousness knows that everyone and everything has its perfect place in this abundant universe. The creative intelligence has a special plan for everyone. Know that your good will come to you in the perfect time and in the perfect way.

Competition, jealousy, and judgment of others are negative and unproductive habits that keep us stuck in limitation. We have no need for competition because we each have our own gift to give. We need not be jealous of each other. On the contrary, by supporting and helping each other, we help heal ourselves and our planet.

By operating with a consciousness of abundance, we see that we gain nothing by fighting others. In fact, we have everything to gain by helping and cooperating with one another. This attitude is the essence of true prosperity.

Prosperity Law #34
I Rejoice in the Fortune of Others

Jealousy and envy stem from poverty consciousness; we fear that someone else is taking our share and that nothing will be left for us. This type of deprivation thinking is unproductive and will hold you back from becoming truly prosperous. When you entertain feelings of envy and jealousy, you are reinforcing a perception of scarcity—and that can only work against you.

Everything happens for a reason. Choose to view other people's happiness as a sign, an omen, that you are headed in the right direction. Take joy in hearing of their good fortune. This attitude expands your capacity to receive abundance, and opens your heart.

When we look at the world with a prosperity consciousness, we can see that this planet has enough for everyone. We need not fear, for as long as we are confident and follow the Universal Laws, prosperity is on our path. Always affirm that all your endeavors are working out perfectly, for the best, and that abundance is available to us all.

Jealousy rarely affects other people;
it only succeeds in tightening your own heart.
Your personal fortune is drawing nearer;
otherwise, you wouldn't be hearing about theirs.
Be glad for the success of others.
The universe has enough for everyone.

Activity: *I Rejoice*

Think about someone you know who has experienced some form of success in his or her life recently. Take a moment to picture this person in your mind. Mentally send this person your love and joy.

Now, take some time to write a note congratulating this person and conveying your good wishes. If you wish, send this letter simply to let your friend know you are happy for his or her success. This activity puts you in the loving space of rejoicing in another's fortune. You will notice a shift, perhaps a feeling of expansion, in the area around your heart. And you will find that you are able to accept more good into your own life as well.

Record this experience in your journal.

Prosperity Law #35
I Choose My Response with Love

We often react to our environment without thinking. Depending on our given mood, we may have a variety of automatic responses to any unplanned situation. Often, our immediate response is a negative one.

We can be more mindful of our reactions by being aware of the energy we carry inside ourselves. We can learn to stay in a loving space so that when difficulties arise, we are better equipped to handle them in a loving, more productive way.

Love is a special energy. It is more than just an emotion. Love has the power to heal and to transform. Indeed, love is the greatest force in the universe, a force that connects us all.

Make the energy of love your natural response. By choosing love, you are activating a powerful, universal force in your life and moving yourself towards true prosperity.

*You become master of your destiny when you
choose your response to a difficult situation
rather than blindly reacting to it.
Tap into your personal power
by asking yourself how you would like to respond.*

Activity: *A Loving Choice*

Try this activity with any automatic reaction that you wish to transform into a loving response.

1. Think of a situation that triggers feelings of annoyance, irritation, discomfort, or anger.

2. Step back and watch the situation in your mind's eye as if it is happening in the present. What is your typical reaction to this situation?

3. Now, list at least three positive benefits you could receive from this situation if you looked at it from a different angle.

4. Allow the awareness of these benefits to change your reaction to the situation; in other words, think of a response you can have as an alternative to the automatic negative reaction that would yield a more loving result.

For instance, here are three benefits you might glean from job hunting:

- Discovering strengths you didn't know you had
- Meeting interesting people and increasing your network
- Gaining confidence

New response to job hunting: Excitement, anticipation, adventure, feeling that a whole new world is opening up.

And here are three benefits you could get from dealing with a difficult person:

- Practicing composure, compassion, and patience
- Learning to speak your mind in a diplomatic way
- Learning not to take what others say personally

New response to a difficult person: Calmness, assertiveness, confidence, and self-love.

Practice this activity regularly to transform your responses.

Prosperity Law #36
I Allow Others to Be Who They Are

The Biblical saying "Judge not, lest thyself be judged" is related to Universal Law. Everything you put out into this universe comes back to you.

When you judge others, you are actually judging yourself; you are merely projecting your negative attitude outwards. You are holding up a one-dimensional standard that doesn't necessarily consider all factors involved, so your perspective suffers. When we look at others without compassion, we ultimately end up doing the same to ourselves.

"Do not judge a man before you have walked a mile in his moccasins" is an old Native American saying. Remember, you may not be aware of all the factors involved regarding the circumstances of another. Only one power is great enough to know the whole situation, and that's not you. Other people may be learning lessons that you do not understand.

Accepting others without judgment is a big step along the way to accepting yourself. You don't have to agree with what others are doing; just focus on your own actions, and do the best *you* can. A non-judgmental attitude and self-acceptance are both crucial for a prosperous life filled with joy.

Don't judge others or criticize what they do with their
money. Stop all gossip. Focus on changing yourself, not others.
Accept other people, and allow them to be who they are,
and you will experience more freedom
and self-acceptance in your own life.

Activity: *Understanding Others*

Are you judging someone negatively? Or is there someone you resent? Picture this person in your mind's eye. Detach your feelings about the person, and see him or her going through an average day.

Watch this person as if he or she was someone you didn't know. See him or her in mundane, everyday activities such as brushing teeth, putting on shoes, or doing the dishes. This helps to gain distance and to see the person more objectively.

If you are in a troubling situation with him or her, affirm that "everything is working out perfectly." Let go of anger or worry. Try to imagine the person enveloped in love and light. This can be difficult, but it is effective.

Realize that there is no way for you to understand any person completely. Each of us has many facets. Though you think you may know someone and that your judgments are justified, you have only just scratched the surface. No one can truly know another person unless you have lived her life and walked in her shoes.

Prosperity Law #37

My Honesty Brings Me Great Fortune

This above all: To thine own self be true.
And it must follow, as the night the day,
That thou cans't not be false to any man.
—*Shakespeare*

When we act with honesty, we send out a message of trust to the universe. If we feel we need to cheat, we send out a message of fear: we do not trust our higher spiritual power, which has our greater good in mind.

Dishonesty keeps us from our dreams. Dishonesty blocks and dampens our energy. When we are dishonest, we may think we are pulling the wool over someone else's eyes, but this act actually harms us. We must live with integrity to all parts of our being.

If you listen to your inner voice, you will hear if you are following your true path or if you are attempting to be deceptive—to yourself as well as to others. If you are on your true path, things fall into place naturally, and you have no need for deceit.

Check within your own heart to see how you feel about your actions, your intentions, and your direction in life. Abundance that comes from truth and integrity brings you and those around you love and joy.

When you tell yourself that you must cheat to receive
wealth, you are sending a message to the universe
that you feel unworthy of real prosperity.
Money acquired through honest endeavors
will provide you with joyful abundance.

☞

Activity: *Honesty Meditation*

I trust in the universe to supply what I need.

I receive with a clear heart.

I am creating abundance through love and service,

with honesty and integrity,

enriching my life, enriching the lives of those around me.

The world is my garden of plenty.

Whatever things are true, whatever things are noble,

whatever things are just, whatever things are pure,

whatever things are lovely,

whatever things are of good report,

if there is any virtue

and if there is anything praiseworthy—

meditate on these things.

—Phillipians 4:8

12.

Opening Yourself to Abundance

It's a funny thing about life,
if you refuse to accept anything but the best,
you very often get it.

—W. Somerset Maugham

Reform any negative opinions you may have about money. There is nothing pious about poverty or scarcity thinking. Remember, money can be used to make positive changes in our world. As Reverend Ike said, "You can't help the poor by being one of them!"

We give money value and meaning with our thoughts, actions, and intentions. Choose to make money an abundant and positive part of your life. We help ourselves as well as others by developing a strong prosperity consciousness and by using our money in productive ways.

Bringing prosperity into your life is much more simple when you feel deserving. Feeling deserving of prosperity creates a healthy self-image that includes a good relationship with money.

The universe is unlimited. The more receptive you are to good, the easier it is for your prosperity to arrive. Know that you are worthy of the best, and start allowing unlimited prosperity into your life.

Prosperity Law #38
I Now Accept My Rightful Abundance

Prosperity is natural, and it is natural for us to prosper in all ways, including financially. But since much of our society attaches a negative connotation to money, we often project negative qualities onto people who have a lot of money. We become suspicious of those who are rich, and we think that being poor is pious.

If you think that money is bad and that only bad people have money, you will naturally push money away. Yet truthfully, just as some rich people are bad, some poor people are bad as well. This has less to do with the amount of money one has and more to do with one's character.

Louise Hay says, "If people are starving in this world, it is not because of a lack of money. It is because of a lack of love."

When more good people have money, money will be used in more positive and productive ways. See yourself as a good person who can and will do marvelous things with your money.

Let go of any sense of guilt you may feel
about having a lot of money.
Money can help you realize your highest aspirations.
You may sabotage your success unless you realize
that it is natural and right for you to prosper.

Activity: *Special Delivery*

Close your eyes, and imagine receiving in the mail a gold box tied with a golden ribbon. You open this package and find it filled with one-hundred dollar bills. This box represents the potential of creating an abundance of good and positive things.

Breathe in a feeling of acceptance and gratitude for this gift, and see yourself enjoying and sharing this abundance with others. Feel your gift of love and abundance enriching your life and the lives of those around you. Visualize yourself and others smiling and content.

Notice if you are experiencing any negative thoughts or feelings during this activity; they may signify a resistance toward having an abundance of money. These feelings of resistance can subtly push prosperity away from you.

Practice accepting this gift of money with love and joy, and allow yourself to feel thankful, deserving, and generous.

Record any observations in your journal.

Prosperity Law #39
I Am Open to All Channels to Receive

The creative intelligence can manifest your abundance in infinite ways. You have no way of anticipating what truly wonderful things are on their way into your life.

The abundance of the universe has many potential channels that it can take to get to you; you may not be aware of them all at this time. If you focus on only one channel for prosperity, for example, a job, you may not be seeing additional opportunities that are open to you. Something may even come from a channel you never anticipated.

Let go of wondering how you will receive your good. Even if you think things look impossible at the moment, all you need do is to keep the faith patiently and persistently. Receive all the prosperity the universe has to offer with an attitude of freedom and openness. Know that your highest good is being created for you *right now.*

*The infinite universe will find magical ways
to bring your abundance to you.
Stay open to all channels so that you don't limit your supply.
Your prosperity may come to you from a
totally unexpected source,
and often in a way much better than you imagined.*

Activity: *Receiving Your Unlimited Good*

Imagine yourself standing in a lush field of the greenest grass looking up to the bright blue sky. The brilliant sun streams with golden rays that are turning into gold flakes above your head and gently raining down on you.

Spread your arms wide open towards the sun, and accept all the prosperity that is flowing over you. Imagine the gold rain representing everything good in your life. Luck and abundance are streaming down on you like manna from heaven.

Joyfully take it all in, knowing that there is more here than you, or anyone else, could ever use in your entire life, and that you deserve all this prosperity the universe has to give. Breathe in and fully receive this abundance into your life with gratitude and joy. *Record any observations in your journal.*

The future holds promises of mysterious good.

Anything can happen over night.

—Florence Scovel Shinn

Prosperity Law #40
I Expect Profitable Surprises

Look to each day with joy and promise. Happy expectancy fills your mind with magic and wonder. This state of being creates miracles in your life.

We often go through our days expecting only the negative to occur, yet every good thing is always possible. Murphy's Law, a running joke in our society, states, "If anything can go wrong, it will." This may seem true among the frustrated masses. However, it is this frame of mind which sets us up for receiving less than we otherwise might.

If you catch yourself thinking a limiting thought, just release it. Say to yourself, "I expect profitable surprises!" And feel the excitement and anticipation of their arrival.

Prosperity thinking means getting out of your own way and allowing the good to flow in. Expecting unexpected but profitable surprises opens the door for all prosperous possibilities to occur.

Look for daily prosperity demonstrations.
Expect to receive unplanned money,
and make a mental note of it when it appears.
Augment this exercise with thankfulness, and you will be
clearing the path for more prosperity to come into your life.

Activity: *Miracles Pages*

Keep a section in your Prosperity Journal to record unexpected abundance and profitable surprises that appear in your life. Be sure to write down every miracle you receive. You may think you can simply keep them in your memory, but these incidences often slip from our awareness.

When you write down all your unusual synchronicities and serendipitous occurrences, you will be able to look back in your journal and have the thrilling experience of seeing how much of your life really *is* guided by the hand of God.

Prosperity Law #41
I Believe in Myself and My Unlimited Potential

In fables, a rainbow in the sky is a fortuitous sign to follow. The pot of gold coins at the end of the rainbow is a symbol of the seeker's dreams.

But real rainbows are refractions of light which stay in the sky and appear to move as you move. If you chase a real rainbow, you will never reach the end. Yet the rainbow is a beautiful sight in itself and is exciting to find and follow.

Your dreams inspire you to chase the rainbow. Your goal, symbolized by the pot of gold coins, spurs you onto the path.

As you follow your rainbow, you discover strengths you never knew you had. You find deep within you the greatness that is untouchable: your own inner beauty. And so you are, indeed, made richer by following your rainbow.

A rainbow is inside you waiting to be discovered. Use your dreams and desires as signposts and clues as to what you are capable of achieving. Remember that God (or your higher spiritual power) never gives you a dream without the inner resources and the wherewithal to achieve it.

Feel confident about your ideas and abilities.
You have deep resources of untapped inner strength.
Believe in your power to change,
and become the person you've always wanted to be.

Activity: *A Letter of Love*

Do you have a talent for music, dancing, or the arts? Do you have a special way of talking to people and soothing them or putting them at ease? Or do you have a gift for really listening to others? Are you a great writer or speaker? What do you love to do? How can you use your special gifts to help others?

Write a heartfelt letter to yourself from the great creative intelligence about the gifts It gave you and how It wants you to use them.

Be still, and receive this letter of love from your higher spiritual power. Listen, and write from your heart.

Below is an example.

Dear_____,

I have given you special talents in the areas of _____, and I am counting on you to contribute to humanity by _____.

I appreciate you for being_____, and I thank you for the wonderful gifts you have already given, as well as those you are about to offer.

...Continue to listen, and write your letter.

Prosperity Law #42
I Like Who I Am and Who I Am Becoming

Too often we tear ourselves down by being unsupportive of ourselves. If a close friend or relative acted this way, we would certainly not put up with it. So why do we accept this from ourselves? You will be much happier and more productive when you treat yourself as you would your dearest friend.

Spend time acknowledging your good traits. Build yourself up. You are the one who is going to be by your side your entire life, so make your relationship with yourself a rewarding one. Practice being your own best friend.

Consider what you like about yourself. Are you a good person? Are you creative? Have you recently done something exceptionally kind for someone?

Bringing these good points to light helps you to glow inwardly. You become stronger and more resolved to be, do, and have what you desire. Focus on your best so that you can be your best.

In order to succeed fully in life,
you must like who you are now.
Instead of criticizing yourself when you look in the mirror,
say to yourself, "I like who I am," and mean it.
Don't underestimate the power of this simple exercise.

Activity: *Self-Appreciation*

We get powerful feedback when we do our positive affirmations in the mirror. The mirror not only shows you what you look like on the outside, but it also reflects back to you what is going on inside your mind and heart.

Next time you are in front of a mirror, look yourself in the eyes, and notice your reaction. Is your first inclination to focus on something you don't like and to put yourself down for it?

Just notice what thoughts go through your head and how they make you feel inside. This can be difficult for some people to do. If your reaction to this activity is negative, that can be very telling as to how you treat yourself.

Whenever you look in the mirror, make sure the first thing you say to yourself is something like this: "I like myself and who I am becoming."

Try this activity: Stand in front of the mirror and say to yourself, "(Your name), I accept you, and I love you, exactly the way you are." Keep saying this until you begin to believe it—and until you begin to feel it. Allow yourself time to grow into this exercise.

The tendency to be hard on yourself will keep prosperity away from you. If you truly want joyful prosperity in your life, you cannot treat yourself like some critical parent. You are the person who lives inside your mind, so you might as well be your own cheering squad.

Take this opportunity to look at yourself again but now more lovingly. Tell your image in the mirror, "I love you and accept you, *no matter what.*" Keep saying it until you *mean* it.

If you find that you are criticizing yourself in any way, just stop. Refuse to criticize yourself anymore.

You must put an end to any type of destructive criticism and vow to support yourself. This is essential to your well being and growth. Do not leave the mirror until you have experienced some self-approval. Insist that you accept yourself exactly the way you are.

If you have trouble accepting any part of your body—or all of it—you may want to take some special time to focus on that particular part and work on loving it.

Think of the wonderful future you are moving towards and the positive changes you are making in your life now.

In the future, whenever you look at yourself or find yourself thinking critically, mentally send yourself love and acceptance, and then focus on feeling good about yourself and thinking positively.

Prosperity Law #43
I See Myself As a Success

Most of us tend to focus on what's wrong with ourselves rather than on what's right. You are what you believe yourself to be, so let us focus on building a winning self-image. Remember, what you concentrate on expands.

Success is an inward journey rather than an outward display. Success has more to do with your self-worth and inner resolve than with your achievements. When you see yourself as a success, other people sense your strength and self-esteem and treat you accordingly.

Believing in yourself brings mighty forces to your aid. Focus on your strengths in each moment, and you will realize the great energy within.

Today is a new day. The past does not equal the future. Regardless of your background, you can create personal success. When you apply the Universal Laws of Prosperity to your life, you are accessing incredibly powerful tools.

Whatever obstacles you believe you face,
others have overcome even greater challenges.
Wherever you are right now is of little consequence.
What really matters is the attitude you possess
and the way you approach life.

Activity: *My Successes and My Strengths*

You are stronger and more successful than you realize. Chances are you have probably overcome considerable hurdles in the past. Reflect on some of the times you have done extraordinarily well, and become acquainted with your successes and your strengths.

Use the example below to create a list of seven or more of your successes, big or small. Go back as far in the past as you like. Next, write out at least seven of your personal strengths.

Record your answers in your journal.

My Successes:	My Strengths:
1. Graduated	1. Compassion
2. Paid-off loan	2. Persistence
3. Made three new friends	3. Resourcefulness
4. Learned to meditate	4. Insight
5. Started exercising	5. Humor
6. Started a business	6. Kindness
7. Quit smoking	7. Creativity

Do what you love.

Do what makes your heart sing,

and never do it for the money.

Seek ye first the kingdom of Heaven,

and the Maserati will get here

when it's supposed to.

—Marianne Williamson

13.

Following a Higher Vision

Most of us have spent so much time doing what we think we *should* do that we have lost part of our souls. We win back our souls when we realize our purpose, create a higher vision to follow, and use our work and accomplishments for the betterment of our families, our society, and ourselves.

Our goal in this chapter is to help you discern what you really want in your life so that you can begin to focus on it and draw it into your world. Remember, what you concentrate on expands, so let us discover what you want to create.

Reflecting on what you want in life will bring you closer to knowing what your purpose is. Your innermost desires will be your guiding light, and your goals will become your beacon. Allow joy to be your compass.

The rewards for listening to your heart and following your dreams are infinite. You become stronger and grow into the person you were meant to be. You accomplish those things you are here on this earth to accomplish. But most of all, you develop a personal relationship with your higher self, and you experience the depths of your spiritual nature.

Prosperity Law #44
I Have Clearly Defined Goals

The process of defining your goals is as individual as you are. The main criteria to remember are to listen to your heart and to be true to yourself.

You do not have to know *how* your prosperity will come to you; you only need to define what it is you want. Once you have done this, you can create goals to guide you on your path.

Your dreams are your destiny. When you follow your destiny, the entire universe conspires to help you. Eleanore Roosevelt said, *"You must do the thing you think you cannot do."*

When you feel doubtful or worried, confidently keep your visions of success in the forefront of your mind, and withdraw any energy you may be expending on fear or dread.

Reach farther than you think you can. You enlist the aid of the creative intelligence when you go beyond your perceived limitations. The creative force wants to help you manifest your dreams.

In the following pages, you will learn simple yet powerful techniques for making your dreams and goals reality.

Clearly defined goals are the most effective way
to put your request into the universe.
The universe will deliver when it knows what you want.
Hold your image vividly in mind,
and be as specific as you can.

Activity A: *What Do You Want?*

Most people focus all their attention on what they don't want in life, and so they very often get it. By completing the activities in this chapter, you will be able to decipher clearly the direction in which you want to steer your life. When you know what you want, you can call it into being. First we will focus on physical things, since they are often the easiest and most obvious to identify.

Make a list of things you need and want in your life. Make an exhaustive list; this helps you get a more complete idea of your vision.

Here you can include anything, for example, a job, career, house, car, relationship, or a vacation.

Use your Prosperity Journal for your answers.

• Things I need...

• Things I want...

You are not creating these lists because you want to emphasize what is lacking in your life, quite the opposite. You attract that on which you focus, so lovingly create these lists as if you are filling out an order form.

Whether you choose to approach this activity slowly and pensively or swiftly and impulsively is fine. You don't need to experience stress over writing your answers. Just be sure to complete these and the other activities in this guidebook truthfully and accurately so you will get the most out of this program.

Activity B: *One Year*

You have just been told by your doctor that you have a rare, incurable disease. You will not be in any pain, but you only have one year to live. *What will you do with this year?*

Record your answer in your journal.

Activity C: *My Values*

This is a two-part list. For the *first* list, write out ten or more of your most important values. You may want to look at your answer from Activity B, *One Year*, for insight or clues. Values are intangible qualities, in other words, things that cannot be touched. For example:

My Values:

Love, compassion, respect, health, honesty, joy, freedom, security, self-esteem, adventure, family, friendship, creativity, peace of mind, spirituality, achievement, happiness, gratitude, intimacy, passion, fun, contribution, purpose.
Now write your own list of ten values in your journal.

For the second list, look over all the values you just identified, and number them in the order of their importance to you. Then, next to each value you listed, write a description of a sentence or two defining what the word means to you. We will refer back to this list to help you incorporate your values into your life goals. *Below is an example:*

1. Love-*Giving, receiving, feeling love; acting from a loving space.*

2. Health-*Experiencing good balance in mind, body, spirit, emotions.*

3. Relationships-*Being together, mutual support, unconditional love.*

4. Spirituality-*Being in the silence, asking for guidance, listening.*

4. Compassion-*Understanding the pain of other beings, serving others.*

5. Peace of mind-*Feeling grounded and connected to my spirit, joy.*

6. Integrity-*Honoring myself, saying what I mean, being sincere.*

7. Self-Esteem-*Loving and feeling good about myself, confidence.*

8. Adventure-*Fully being in the now, excitement, aliveness.*

Activity D: *Closer to the Heart*

Next we will place our focus on the desires that are closest to our hearts. Do you remember your childhood dreams? What were some of your favorite activities? And what do you love to do now? The important point of this exercise is to record what brings you joy.

Answer the following questions. Don't worry about how realistic or practical your answers may seem. Don't judge what you are writing; just make sure that you loved what you were doing at the time.

Record your answers in your journal.

· When I look back in my life to the times I was happiest, this is what I was doing…

· When I was a child, these are the things I wanted to be when I grew up…

· This is what gets me the most energized…

· I get so absorbed in this activity that I forget time…

· This is what I want to create in my life right now…

· I remember when…*(talk about a clear memory of joy as a child.)*

My life is my message.

—Mahatma Ghandi

Prosperity Law #45
Doing What I Love Serves Others

Anybody can be great,
because greatness is determined by service.
—Martin Luther King, Jr.

When you choose your life goals from a joyful and inwardly centered space, you have a richer sense of self-worth and deserving. Then you realize that work, money, and success do not *bring* happiness; they are *expressions of* happiness.

Have you ever considered the possibility that your dreams and passions are connected with your personal mission in life? That if you do not develop your natural talents and follow your dreams, you may miss your purpose for being on this planet? That if you do not achieve your mission, your journey here may be incomplete?

Your life and potential gifts to the world are uniquely your own. No one has the combination of traits and talents that you have. No one but you can give the gifts that you are here to share. By sharing and developing your talents, you reward yourself and those around you immeasurably.

Loving your work gives you a sense of happiness, excellence, and excitement. Let love and joy guide you in your search for your life's work.

Selfless service is the highest form of work.
It is best accomplished by doing what you love
and bringing it into the world
for the benefit and enjoyment of others.

Activity: *Joyful Abundance*

When we are joyful in our work, we are most productive. We are also in the best position to give gracefully and lovingly to the world. Joy is a signal that you are doing the type of work that you are meant to do.

Always remember, this universe is naturally abundant, and when you *know* what you want, you can *have* it—or something even better than you can imagine!

Complete these sentences. You don't have to think hard; just write down what comes into your mind on first impulse. This activity is meant to be fun. Do not try to be practical here: let your imagination soar.

· If I could do, be, and have anything, I would...

· Before I die, I will...

· These are some of the things I would like to change about my life right now...

· These are the careers that have excited me in the past...

· This is what I would spend the next year doing if I knew I couldn't fail...

· The things I love most are...

(pets, activities, hobbies, travel, anything!)

· If I didn't worry about money, this is what I would do with my life...

Record your answers in your journal.

You may not think that the world needs you,
but it does.

For you are unique,
like no one that has ever been before
or will come after.

No one can speak with your voice, say your piece,
smile your smile, or shine your light.

No one can take your place,
for it is yours alone to fill.

If you are not there to shine your light,
who knows how many travelers will lose
their way as they try to pass by
your empty place in the darkness?

—Unknown

Prosperity Law #46

My Life Has Purpose and Meaning

At times, we all feel a little lost and disheartened, but this does not mean that our lives are meaningless. Everything happens to us for a reason. Despite the pain we encounter from time to time, we each have a purpose for being here.

Our tribulations fuel our inner growth. Moreover, the lessons we learn from hard times often help us to develop true compassion for others in similar situations.

Whether or not you realize it, you are a vital link in the chain. The cobwebs of connectedness thread us all together. As one part of the web stirs, no matter how small, a movement is felt throughout.

You are just as important as anyone else on this planet, no more and no less. Realize this truth, and open yourself to the possible answers as to what your life's mission could be. The job(s) you are here to do are vital to your growth and to the evolution of our planet.

When your purpose is clear to you, you awaken each day with a fullness in your heart and the awareness that your being alive is making a positive difference in our world.

Everything in this incredible universe is
perfectly orchestrated and finely tuned.
We are all individual parts of a whole, and as such, we are one.
There is a master plan. There are no accidents.
There is meaning and harmony in everything that happens.

Activity: *My Purpose*

This activity is designed to help you determine your purpose at this time in your life. Your purpose is similar to a mission, something important you are here on this planet to accomplish.

When you formulate your purpose, it must be something that is infinite, something that you cannot finish. For instance, you could describe your purpose in any of the following ways:

· *I facilitate healing in myself and others.*

· *I am a channel for light and peace on this planet.*

· *Fostering love in myself and others.*

· *I impart compassion and protection for animals.*

· *Inspiring hope and joy in myself and others.*

Your life's purpose is something you can remember every day, and you can live it in each moment. But it is something you cannot finish. For example, "To build a house" is not a purpose. It can be a goal but not a purpose, because it is something that can be finished.

Or suppose you want to be a doctor. You would not state your purpose as "to be a doctor" or "to fix broken bones." Rather, "Healing hearts and souls through the process of healing the body." Your ultimate purpose is your intention and the action you can take to increase the good and the positive energy in the situation, thus bringing more light into the world.

When you are discovering your purpose, listen to your heart. If a word, thought, or concept makes your heart jump for joy, you have a clear signal that it is related to your purpose.

The following three steps will guide you in discovering your purpose:

- **First**, choose any verb that rings true for you, such as *healing, restoring, induce, protect, develop, encouraging, empowering, motivating, evoke, nurture, enliven, assist.*

- **Second**, add a concept that inspires you, for example, *love, joy, courage, serenity, fun, freedom, hope, faith, light, or strength.*

- **Third**, end the sentence by saying "in myself and others" or "on the planet" or something to that end.

Your purpose is your gift to the world as well as to yourself. It is your way of uplifting the energy on this planet.

People get caught up thinking that they just have one special title or role. Each one of us can actually have as many as seven to ten right livelihoods. Yet we can always bring our life's purpose to the job we are presently doing.

Carry your purpose in your heart, and know that your contribution is vital. Record your purpose in your journal.

A person writing at night may put out the lamp,

but the words he has written will remain.

It is the same with the destiny we create

for ourselves in this world.

—Shakyamnni

14.

Designing Your Prosperity Plan

Through the process of dreaming about the things you love and what you want out of life, you clarify the details of the prosperous destiny you are creating for yourself. Defining your dreams can be great fun and helps lay the groundwork for successfully transforming your life goals into reality.

When we create plans to achieve the things that get us excited about life, our goals become special gems that cause us to greet the day with delighted anticipation. We wake up motivated to joyfully take the steps that lead us to realizing our dreams.

When we resolutely follow the Universal Laws of Prosperity, our dreams manifest in our lives in the perfect way. We also experience the special sense of fulfillment that comes from knowing that we are directing our lives (in partnership with our higher spiritual power) and creating the joy, beauty, and abundance that is our divine right.

So let us forge ahead and confidently declare our most cherished dreams, and then we will build a plan that will help them become reality.

Prosperity Law #47

I Am Earning an Excellent Income Doing What I Love

You were given a specific set of talents, desires, and abilities for a reason: When you wish to do a particular type of work, a gift is always on the path for you to give to others. You are meant to have satisfying work that benefits others and nurtures your soul. And you will be rewarded on many levels for following your dreams.

Affirm that you are receiving excellent pay for work that you love to do. You don't even have to know what kind of work that is right now. The universe will let you know. Signposts on your journey of life tell you where your true purpose lies. Doors will open for you easily, and the path will unfold naturally, telling you that you are on the right track. Be open and receptive to these clues.

Let your heart be your guide, and pay close attention to the things that bring you joy. That which you love to do is connected to your calling.

Remember to stay open to how you can use your calling to serve others. This is what will bring you ultimate fulfillment and satisfaction.

To be truly prosperous, you must follow your heart.
Prosperity includes leading the life you want to lead,
doing what you love to do.
Applying this philosophy to your career
creates excellence and brings joy into the world.

A Bold and Daring Adventure

Sometimes we are afraid to acknowledge what we really want because then we can no longer deny to ourselves what our dreams are: We will actually have to go out into the world and *create* them.

Following your dreams takes everything you have inside of you, but this doesn't mean you need to struggle. On the contrary, you are discovering the highest meaning and purpose for your life, and you are partnering with the higher creative power to bring it into being.

Helen Keller once said, "Life is either a bold and daring adventure, or nothing." She was an incredible human being, as well as a famous writer and speaker. She wrote and published her first book at age twenty-two, despite being blind and deaf.

You can have an exciting life in which you pursue your dreams and become all that you can be, or you can have a "safe" existence, where you can be careful and guarded but probably unfulfilled. Which will you choose?

Activity A: *Reflections*

Imagine for a moment that you are 99 years old and you are reflecting back over your life. What are you especially proud of? What was most important to you? What were your contributions to humanity and the planet? How did you live your life? Did you learn to love? What dreams did you realize? How did you help others?

Write about the reflections of your life in your prosperity journal.

☞

Blueprint for Prosperity

The last activity, *Reflections*, helped you to imagine the wonderful life you are about to create. As you complete the next activity, *Designing Your Prosperity Plan,* you become more specific by creating ideal scenarios. You will now begin fashioning a detailed vision of a life you love.

Do not limit yourself by worrying about how you are going to achieve your dreams. First you must know *what* you truly want to create. We will discover the *how* in following chapters, which contain powerful techniques for realizing your dreams.

Review your responses to the activities in Chapter 13, *Following a Higher Vision*, to gain clues about what your answers might be in this next activity. Acknowledge every aspiration that gives you joy, whether or not you believe it is possible for you at this time. And don't limit yourself by thinking small. Remember to "Slip through the Gap" and to think in terms of possibilities. Be sure not to force answers that you may not have. They will come in time.

The following activity consists of a list of tangible goals and also intangible goals such as *Self-Image, Relationship with Money, The Present Moment.* The purpose of the intangible goals is to provide you with answers to questions such as "What do I want to feel after I've reached the outer goals?" and "What is the positive effect I want to have on others?" We call these "Ultimate Goals" because when you are moving toward external goals, you are ultimately striving to attain success in these inner realms as well. We usually don't think about these untouchable goals much, but including them in your list is essential for happiness and fulfillment.

Activity B: *Designing Your Prosperity Plan*

Create an ideal scenario for the areas below. Listen to your intuition, and write whatever feels authentic. Your answers to this activity are not set in stone, and you may change, add to, or adjust them as you come up with new ideas. Also, feel free to add categories that you feel are missing.

You don't have to work on all these areas at once, you can just explore one or two at a time. Work at your own pace.

Self-Image: *What kind of a relationship do you want to have with yourself? How do you wish to treat yourself (with love, respect, kindness?) How do you want to see yourself? How do you want to feel about yourself? Really spend time thinking this through. A positive self-image is vital for happiness. Be your own best friend.*

Health: *Health is wealth. Do you want more energy? Would you like to have a toned, healthy body? Would you like to be free of ailments? What types of physical activity do you enjoy?*

Home: *Your home is your sanctuary. Is your home a nurturing, comforting, inspiring place? How do you want it to feel and look? What changes would you like to make? Do you want to have more meaningful decorations and pictures? What is your ideal home environment?*

Relationships: *Would you like more caring friends? Excellent relations with your family? A loving mate? Deeper intimacy? Good business and work relationships? How would you like to be seen in the eyes of others? List and describe your important relationships.*

The Present Moment: *Don't forget about the all-important moment. Now is all you have. How do you want to experience it? As you go through your life, how do you want to feel? Optimistic? Happy? Loving? Purposeful? Empowered? Connected? Confident?*

Finances: *How much money would you like to earn? How do you want to earn it? How much do you need to have saved to feel secure? How much discretionary income do you want? Would you like to create financial prosperity joyfully and honestly, with full integrity? Do you want to invest, donate, or even start a charity?*

Relationship with Money: *How do you want to feel about money and your finances? Would you like to feel confident, peaceful, secure, prosperous, joyful?*

Rewarding Career / Job: *In what area(s) do you want to excel? What are your interests? What thrills you? What is your desired work environment like? How do you want to serve the planet?*

Self-Development: *What strengths, qualities, and personality traits do you want to develop in yourself? What special knowledge or skills would you like to learn? What would achieving your full potential look like?*

Gifts to the World: *What gifts do you want to give to the world through your job or career? Are there also other ways you would like to contribute to the good of the planet, for instance, through a favorite hobby, activity, or volunteer work?*

Spirituality: *How might you feel more fully connected to your higher power and have a closer relationship with your spiritual self? Do you want the experience that your life is full of miracles and that you are being guided by the hand of God? Would you like to feel the sacredness and mystery of life? Do you want to live in the flow?*

Recreation: *We often forget to enjoy life or just relax. How do you like to play? Describe your ideal scene for any or all of the following types of fun: sports, hobbies, artistic expression, travel, vacations. All recreational elements of life renew the spirit.*

What to do if you are unsure of the answers...

Most of us haven't been taught how to discover our ideal livelihood or think about the things we'd love to be doing. We haven't been told that we're worthy of following our dreams or that working at what we love is a productive approach to life. This may make answering some of the previous questions somewhat difficult.

If you feel unsure about any of your answers, a simple way to discover what you want is to make a list of what you *don't* want; then just write out the opposite of those things you don't want.

You can also put an inquiry into the universe, and allow the perfect answers to come to you in their own time. A powerful and effective way to do this is to meditate with the question or affirmation in mind. Make space for the answer— it may come immediately, and it may not.

You may need to meditate once, or for several days in a row. Be patient. Listen, stay open, and watch for clues in your daily life. Confidently trust that the perfect answer will come when you are ready to receive it. In the meantime, enjoy this current moment and the exciting process of designing your abundant life!

The Birth of HAR-MONEY™

When you ask for guidance with an open heart, you allow room for miracles and synchronicities to occur in your life. You experience a whole new level of awareness, and your life takes on a new dimension of meaning. This is what happened with HAR-MONEY™.

The *HAR-MONEY™ Cards* (see page 23) were initially conceptualized with my dearest friend, Janea Dahl. Several years ago, we began to meet every evening to meditate at dusk for about twenty minutes. We wanted to discover a way to create prosperity while helping others. We asked for guidance and affirmed and visualized prosperity for ourselves, each other, and the world.

On the eighth day of meeting together, I suddenly broke out of the meditation, opened my eyes, and exclaimed, "I have an idea. Let's put prosperity affirmations on money!" Without missing a beat, Janea opened her eyes and replied, "And we'll call it HAR-MONEY!"

We continued to meet at dusk each evening, asking for higher guidance and ideas while we developed the HAR-MONEY™ concept.

Secrets to Lifelong Prosperity or as we often refer to it, the HAR-MONEY™ Guidebook, was later created as an companion manual to the *HAR-MONEY™ Cards*. The experience that we shared was magical and filled with meaningful coincidences. Asking for guidance created a whole new adventure for us.

Everything you can imagine is real.

—*Pablo Picasso*

15.

Intentions

Intention is a subtle energy that attracts prosperity. It is an inner *decision* that draws your dreams toward you. It means, "I want this goal, and I fully intend to bring this goal into being."

When you discover something that you truly desire, you will feel a pull urging you to go forward, and the intention to create it will easily follow.

If you say that you want something but do not really intend for it to occur, you create incongruity. This weakens the life force and disperses energy that otherwise would have helped your goal to manifest.

Check to make sure that each ideal scenario you wrote in *Designing Your Prosperity Plan* inspires you. If one does not, then keep exploring in that area until you discover an answer that enlivens your spirit. What are the goals that excite and motivate you? In what areas can you create the most joy for yourself and for those around you while helping to heal and advance humanity?

If you cannot come up with an ideal scenario that is true to your spirit at this time, remember to ask the creative intelligence, and then be open to the answers. There is no rush; the most important thing is that when the answers do come, they speak to your soul.

The Strength of Your Intention

Look at each ideal scenario you wrote for the activity, *Designing Your Prosperity Plan* on page 186, and pay attention to your inner voice or gut feelings. Be sure that the ideal scenario really came from *your* dreams and that you are not just writing it down because it is something someone else wants for you.

For example, maybe your parents told you that they wanted you to be a doctor or lawyer. Or perhaps they wanted you to go into business, but you really want to be in the arts.

Many of us are used to trying to please others. Make sure that you are not doing this with your goals. Also, don't just write something because you think it will *sound* good to other people. Write down what *you* really want.

If you really want the ideal scenario but don't feel quite ready for it to manifest yet, that is fine. You may want to look at the reasons why. Is some sort of fear in the way? If so, ask yourself what the fear is about. Break the goal down into sections, and honestly look at what concerns you. Overcome your fears one at a time, with awareness, insight, and affirmations.

Perhaps you want a portion of what the dream represents but not all of it. In that case, decipher which parts appeal to you, and design your dream accordingly. Or maybe it is just a rough draft and you will find an ideal scenario that fits you better in the near future. Just keep pondering the dream, and its time will come.

Prosperity Law #48

I Fully Intend to Realize My Dreams

The strength of your intention to create something influences how your dreams and goals unfold. Therefore, you want to be clear about what your intentions are. Be sure that they are aligned positively with your goals.

Ask yourself these questions: How much do I want this goal? Am I ready to accept this? Can I see myself having it? The answers let you know how strong your intention is.

Another powerful way we can use the concept of intention to bring our dreams into being is by tapping into a higher (or spiritual) intention. Having a higher intention for a goal helps you feel grounded, purposeful, and present in each moment.

No matter what our goals look like on the outside, there is always an underlying lesson for our soul—what we came into this life to learn. Each one of us has a unique offering, whether it be to serve others, to learn to give and receive, or to simply experience more love and joy in our lives.

In the following activity we will learn to infuse our goals with a higher intention. Discovering a higher intention for one or more of your goals will give you an understanding of the higher purpose behind that goal.

Your intentions create a powerful energy that works
with the creative intelligence to manifest your dreams.
Align your intentions with your goals,
and your dreams will become real.

Activity: *Creating Your Higher Intention*

Creating a higher intention is energizing and will light you up and motivate you when you think about your dream. It lets you pinpoint what is essential to you about your goal and can effectively help you to overcome the fear of moving forward.

People commonly choose to create a higher intention for their job or career, but you can use it for any of your dreams or goals.

To create a higher intention, choose one of your ideal scenarios from *Designing Your Prosperity Plan* on page 186. Think about how you want your dream to manifest.

• What positive effect do you intend to have on others?

• How will realizing your dream improve the world?

• How will it help you grow spiritually?

You may also wish to look at the *My Purpose* exercise on page 178. Your intention may correspond closely with what you wrote as your purpose in that activity.

When you are clear as to what your higher intention is, write a scenario stating this positive idea in affirmation form (first person/present tense). Do this activity with as many of your dreams or goals as you would like. You can make your intention a sentence, a paragraph, or longer.

Your higher intention is like a sacred mission statement.

Here are three examples:

Dream/ Goal:
To write a monthly column for a National Magazine...

Higher Intention:
My articles show people how to invest their money in line with their values and how to prosper while making a difference...

Dream/ Goal:
To be a popular professional musician...

Higher Intention:
The sound of my music inspires and uplifts those who hear it. They leave my performances with a sense of hope, love, and joy...

Dream/ Goal:
To be a high school English teacher.

Higher Intention:
My teaching empowers students to communicate effectively, thus helping them to create stronger and more harmonious relationships...

Now choose one or more of your most important goals and create a higher intention that inspires you.

Record your goal and the higher intention your created for it in your Prosperity Journal.

Obstacles are what you see

when you take your eyes off the goal.

—Helen Keller

16.

A Date with Destiny

When you focus on a goal with the confidence that you can achieve it, your mind begins to think about ways to reach that goal, and obstacles fall by the wayside. But when you stop thinking about the goal and think instead about the reasons why it will be difficult to achieve, obstacles pop up everywhere—some real, some imagined. As a result, you will be less likely to move forward and succeed.

Always keep a positive, optimistic eye on your goal. Follow the Prosperity Laws, and the universe will go to work figuring out how to make it happen for you in the best way possible. When you keep cherished dreams firmly in mind and believe that you will succeed, your mind makes room for those dreams in your life.

In previous chapters you spent time discovering and defining what you want to create in your life. In this next section we will build on those discoveries and transform your ideal scenarios and intentions into positively stated goals.

Prosperity Law #49
I Always Put My Goals in Writing

Almost everything you see that is made by humans was initially a thought in someone's mind. Often, this thought was first written down on paper and then later made in solid form.

Putting your dreams on paper crystallizes them in your imagination and brings you one step closer to creating them. Think of writing down your goals as creating a prosperity blueprint. You are giving the creative intelligence a definite list to go by. When you make your list, you will note the important details and intentions that you would like to manifest.

Once you have them in writing, your dreams are no longer just in your mind: They are now in a form that you can see and hold. Recording your goals on paper will help you to clarify what you want and will work magic in your life.

As you keep your prosperity blueprint in mind, always allow for the best possible outcome to be realized. In other words, do the footwork, but leave the final results up to your higher power.

Your written word has power.
When you put your goals in writing,
include important details and a target date.
Keep your list private.
Be flexible, and modify it as you reach each goal.
Remember to stay open to the best possible outcome.

Activity A: *Turning Dreams into Gold*

If you have completed the activities in Chapter 13, *Following a Higher Vision*, and Chapter 14, *Designing Your Prosperity Plan*, then the following activity will practically write itself!

Look through all your answers from the activities in those chapters, including the things you want and need, your values, your purpose, and your ideal scenarios. You should get a very good idea about what type of life you'd like to have and what goals you want to create.

When you see something specific in those pages that you want to turn into a goal, list it under one of these headings: *Short-Term Goals* or *Long-Term Goals*.

Again, remember not to judge how easy or difficult you think the goal will be to attain. If it is something you dream of, then write it down.

The main guidelines are that each goal is humanly possible and is harmful to no one. Also, as we discussed, be sure it is something you really want, not just what someone else wants you to do or something that might sound good to others. Finally, check to see that your goals do not contradict each other.

Include any important detailed information with your goals. For instance, if you want the perfect job, you may want to specify details such as harmonious work relations, excellent pay, and a fun atmosphere.

Writing out the list of goals that you want to create in your life is the next step in making them your reality!

Here is a sample list of goals. Add descriptions whenever possible:

Short-term goals:

· The perfect job (describe) for excellent pay (how much?)

· A cozy, beautiful place to live (describe)

· A loving relationship with a wonderful person (describe)

· A new car (what make and model?)

· A confident and loving self-image

· Peace of mind and a secure relationship with money

· Travel (where, when, how often, with whom?)

· Start working out

· Classes to learn a new skill

Long-term goals:

· A harmonious, happy, and close family life

· A loving spouse (describe qualities that are important to you)

· A successful, exciting career in the field of _____

· An income of $_____ per year

· Savings, assets, and investments of $_____

· To make huge contributions in the areas of _____

· Enough money to be, do, and have what I want

· Excellent health, plenty of energy

· Inner peace, sense of purpose, full enjoyment of the moment

· Lifelong friends who are fun, intelligent, and spiritual

· A loving, supportive relationship with my sister

· Learn to play a musical instrument

Of course we want more out of life than just things. We are also enriched by the personal qualities and character traits we possess. Our personal qualities help us to reach our dreams, enjoy our lives, and contribute to the good of the whole.

Write a list of personal qualities and character traits you would like to cultivate or attain. Be sure to look over your goals from the last page and add any traits you will need in order to accomplish your goals. *Below is a sample list.*

Personal qualities that I want or need:

· Joyful disposition

· Confidence

· Persistence

· Charm

· Creativity

· Patience

· Gentleness

· Positive outlook

· Honesty

· Concentration

· Organization

· Energy

· Self-Respect

· Decisiveness

· Perseverance

· Resourcefulness

Life isn't about finding yourself,

Life is about creating yourself.

—George Bernard Shaw

Activity B: *Affirmative Goals*

Now we will transform each of your goals and personal qualities into powerful affirmations. These affirmations are the building blocks of your prosperity plan.

Be sure your affirmations feel right when you say them. Make them short, sweet, and easy to say.

To make your affirmations most effective, write them in the present tense. Say them as if they are already here.

Do not write, "I will have the perfect job."
Do write, "I *now have* the perfect job."

In addition, if you have specific details that are important to you, include them. For instance,

"I now have the perfect job *working for the Kennedy Group.*"

Also make sure that you state your affirmations positively.

Do not write, "I don't worry about money."
Do write, "*I am confidently* earning a great living."

We create many of our outer experiences first from within. The subconscious mind can't tell the difference between imagination and reality when you are meditating or dreaming. While you sleep, your dreams seem real because your conscious mind is not awake to judge them. When you state an affirmation as if you've already accomplished it and suspend your critical mind (as in meditation), the subconscious mind will not judge what you tell it. Instead, it will go to work in conjunction with the universe to make your affirmation real.

There are two things to aim at in life:

first, to get what you want;

and, after that, to enjoy it.

Only the wisest of mankind achieve the second.

—Logan Pearsall Smith

17.

The Secret of Creating Joyful Abundance

If you have performed all the guidebook activities up to now, you will have discovered and written down your dreams and desires and turned them into goals and affirmations. You now find yourself looking at a list of dreams that cause your heart to jump for joy. In this chapter we are getting ready to make them real.

What ultimately causes your goals to manifest in the perfect way is the quality of emotional energy you put into them. You must infuse your goals with the same quality of energy that you want to experience when you attain them. This prosperity secret attracts your dreams to you in the ideal manner.

Remember, our universe is made up of energy; energy is the commerce of the cosmos. Your vibration (or energy) draws people, things, and situations to you. The type of energy you send into the universe will largely determine the type of experiences you attract into your life.

In this next section we discuss how to energize your goals so that they will be created for you in the best possible way.

Prosperity Law #50
I Am Prosperity

Henceforth I ask not good fortune.
I myself am good fortune.
—Walt Whitman

Focus on the meaning of a word, and your personal energy will rise to match the energy of that word's essence. Allow that energy to occupy your consciousness, and you will draw that word's qualities into your life. In other words, don't just think about prosperity; *be prosperity.*

Prosperity is a magnificent concept, the thought of which can cause us to experience powerfully positive feelings. What does the word *prosperity* awaken in your soul? How does prosperity feel to you?

As you ponder each of your dreams and goals, notice and cultivate the positive feelings they awaken within you. By letting your mind and emotions serenely meditate on the basic essence of words such as *prosperity, joy, success,* and *abundance,* you magnetize their qualities in the perfect way. Tell yourself, "I *Am* Prosperity;" then turn around and *be* it.

Sometimes one word is all it takes.
Consciously place your attention on the word "prosperity."
Allow your mind and emotions to dwell on the qualities and
feelings that this word evokes within you, and you will
gently and surely draw prosperity into your life.

Know What You Really Want

If you want to take a trip around the world, you may be looking to experience freedom, adventure, and excitement—and you think the trip will render these qualities. Or if your goal is to be a millionaire, you may want these riches because you believe a lot of money will give you a feeling of security, independence, and power. Maybe you simply want a spouse to have a regular source of love, comfort, and stability.

But the following information might come as a surprise: taking a trip around the world may *not* give you the experience of freedom, adventure, and excitement, and having a million dollars may *not* give you security or power. Likewise, your spouse may *not* be a continual source of love, comfort, and stability.

What if you went on vacation but were sick the whole time from drinking bad water? All you would want is to be at home cozy in your bed. What if you had a million dollars but worried constantly about losing it? That would not give you the financial security you were looking for. What if you often found yourself fighting bitterly with your spouse? You may feel more lonely than before, when you were single.

These scenarios illustrate why we do not want to focus on just creating *things* (a trip around the world, a million dollars, a partner or spouse). We need to focus on the positive *qualities* or *feelings* we want to experience through having these things—a trip filled with *fun, joy,* and *synchronicity;* our finances adding to our *sense of security* and *well being;* a relationship that is truly *loving* and *intimate.* That way you get what you really want, not just a representation.

Your goals will fall into place—and often in a way much better than you imagined—when you first specify the essences, or qualities, that you desire to experience through achieving those goals.

Prepare your mind to receive

the best life has to offer.

—Ernest Holmes

Activity: *Magical Qualities*

Find a time when you can relax and get comfortable. Look at the list of affirmations you created for the activity on page 203, and select a favorite affirmation to work with. Write this affirmation at the top of a blank page in your journal. Take a few deep breaths, and silently repeat this affirmation.

Use your imagination to experience the qualities you want to realize when you achieve this goal. Visualize the details of your successful endeavor. As the positive feelings rise up within you, write them down underneath your goal.

For example,

Affirmation: *I now have a wonderful job with the perfect pay.*
Qualities: *Service, Teamwork, Creativity, Innovation, Recognition.*

Affirmation: *I am in the perfect relationship with a wonderful person.*
Qualities: *Passion, Love, Happiness, Security, Intimacy, Tenderness.*

Affirmation: *I easily afford a six month trip through Europe.*
Qualities: *Adventure, Fun, Joy, Freedom, Wonder, Beauty, Excitement.*

By listing these qualities, you are giving the creative intelligence important specific details about how you want your goal to manifest. Whenever you think of your affirmation, focus on the qualities you wrote down here. Engaging in activities that will help you experience these qualities *now* will also help to magnetize your goal. Know that the creative force is masterminding your goal for the best possible outcome.

Perform this activity with all the goals and affirmations that are most important to you. **Note:** You may also wish to make a list of positive qualities you want to experience in life and include them under your affirmations wherever appropriate.

To accomplish great things,

we must not only act,

but also dream;

not only plan,

but also believe.

—*Anatole France*

18.

Living Your Dreams

In this chapter you will learn to apply the dynamic art of creative visualization. You will practice experiencing your dreams and goals as if they are real *now*.

The concept of creating your reality in your imagination may at first seem unusual or unlikely. But as you seriously put visualization into practice, you will see results that will convince you to maintain this technique as a vital part of your routine.

We are often unconsciously projecting ourselves into the future, imagining results and influencing outcomes with our expectations. Now we will harness that energy and make sure our visions and projections are positive and are aligned with what we want to create.

Just as you would picture a past or future event in your mind, use the same process to picture your affirmation coming to life. Try to engage as many senses as you can as you repeat your affirmation. See yourself in the scene, hear the sounds around you, feel the feelings and sensations, and smell the smells. Make it real as if it is happening in the present.

The more regularly you apply to your affirmations these simple visualization techniques—and combine them with real emotion and guided action—the more swiftly you will see the outcomes you are looking for.

Prosperity Law #51

I Feel My Dreams Come Alive

First you conceptualize an idea or a dream. Next you breathe life into it with the energy of your imagination and intentions. Then you listen to your intuition and take action. Once you have done these things, you wait patiently and allow your dream to manifest in the perfect way and time.

Emotion is the fuel that ignites your visualizations with vibrancy and life. When you add emotions such as positive expectancy, joy, and excitement to your visualization, your dreams will come alive, first in the ideal and then in the *real*.

You feel your dreams as if they are coming alive in the present, because you can only receive your good in the present. This moment is all you really ever have. The future always becomes the here and now. By imagining that your goals are real using creative visualization, you draw your dreams into your present reality.

It may take time to work up to keeping the positive emotions steady in a visualization. But by practicing visualization and by working through the activities in future chapters that help you release negativity, you will feel clearer. With increased clarity, you will find that creative visualization infused with positive emotion is easy to achieve.

So vibrant is the human spirit that it can have
a truly profound effect on the subconscious mind.
Merely intellectualizing something is not enough.
You must create the feeling within you
that your dreams are coming alive.

Activity A: *The Well of Natural Enthusiasm*

Choose one or more events that happened to you that were particularly filled with joy and excitement, or think of a time when you worked towards something important that you achieved.

If you have a photograph, video, or something that you wrote during that period, now would be a good time to look at it.

Just thinking about those moments may create excitement welling up within you. This is the type of real-life emotional energy you want to create when you are doing your visualizations.

Any time you perform a visualization, allow yourself to be fully present, as if you are in the moment when it is happening.

Practice remembering joy-filled occasions and infusing this vibrant energy into your visualizations. Strive to feel the same natural enthusiasm in your visualizations that you felt during the other great moments of your life.

In your journal, describe your experience of recalling a joyful memory.

Activity B: *Living Your Dream*

Try this *Living Your Dream* technique right now with one of your affirmations from the activity *Magical Qualities* on page 209 in the previous chapter. Look over the qualities you listed for this affirmation. If you wrote an ideal scenario or any other notes that go along with this affirmation, pull those out as well.

What you see in front of you is a detailed, multifaceted description of your dream. You now have a full palate with which to live your dream.

To begin this *Living Your Dream* activity, find a comfortable position, either sitting or lying down, and take several deep breaths. Close your eyes, and silently repeat your affirmation. Picture your ideal scenario, and think of the qualities and feelings that you want to experience along with it.

Remember, in visualization, the past, present, and the future are all one. This is an art that is not bound by time. Therefore, you always experience your visualizations as if they are happening right now, in the present.

Allow yourself to *live your dream* fully in this moment. Feel your excitement while affirming that your dream is real *now*. Vividly imagine the joy of your dream being realized.

In your journal, describe this experience of Living Your Dream.

☞

Guidelines for Performing Your Affirmation Sessions

The following pages provide instructions for saying affirmations on a daily basis. These instructions are guidelines; read them, then do what works best for you. Feel free to modify these guidelines to suit your lifestyle and to fit comfortably into your schedule. It is helpful to create a routine you will be able to stick with over a period of time.

1. To start, select up to eight affirmations you want to work with over the next three weeks.

2. Quietly meditate and repeat these affirmations with feeling three times a day—once in the morning, once in the middle of your day, and once again in the evening. Say these affirmations in the present tense, and feel as if they are already true.

3. During at least one session per day, choose one or more affirmations with which to perform deeper visualizations using the *Living Your Dreams* techniques described in this chapter. Living your dreams with intense feeling at least once a day helps you to focus quality time and energy on your most meaningful goals.

4. Perform this daily affirmation routine for three weeks; then surrender your dreams to the universe, knowing that you've done your part. *After you release your affirmations, select up to eight more to visualize over the next three-week period.*

As a general rule, you will usually see manifestations appear within three months. Simpler dreams may manifest more quickly, while larger dreams can take more time.

By performing these regular affirmation sessions and joyfully visualizing and living your dreams, you are impressing your desires upon the universal mind. After you have released your affirmations to the creative intelligence, continue following up with positive thoughts and appropriate action.

Energizing Your Visualizations

When a visualization is infused with deep emotion, there is no prescribed length of time to hold it; just continue as long as it is fun for you. This type of creative visualization, of feeling your dreams come alive, is usually quite joy-filled for the person performing it and can be something you really look forward to. This is a rejuvenating activity that can be just as productive—if not more so—than your regular work.

The important thing is to see yourself attaining your goal and to experience the pure joy of your triumph. *Feel* the confidence flow throughout your entire body. *Know that you are worthy of your dream.*

If you have any feelings or thoughts of doubt or uncertainty as you say an affirmation, don't resist them. Just tell them lightly, "Thank you for sharing," and gently let them go. Similarly, if you find yourself picturing a negative situation, just release it, and continue to focus on what you want.

The Golden Hour

One of the most powerful times to impress your consciousness with new ideas is in the hour after you wake up. This is called "The Golden Hour" because your mind is usually clear and open to suggestion. The hour before you go to sleep is also extremely effective because you will carry your affirmations into the dream state and etch them onto your subconscious mind. A third great time for an affirmation session is in the middle of the day, when you can take a few moments to relax and to recharge your batteries as well as your dreams.

Loving Persistence

Don't make yourself feel guilty if you miss an affirmation session or two—just pick up where you left off. If you can't do your affirmations three times a day, do them twice or once.

If your schedule or temperament makes creating a routine difficult, affirm and visualize according your ability, and use your intuition to find the best time to surrender your dreams to the universe.

Everyone has different strengths in visualization. Some people are more visual, while others are more auditory. Still others are more adept at feeling. When it comes to mental imagery, don't worry if you have difficulty with any of these modalities. Just use your dominant senses (those that come easiest to you) and make it real for you.

Thank yourself for the time and effort that you are able to commit, and remember to love yourself, make it fun, and keep your dreams close to your heart.

All This or Something Better

When you complete any affirmation or visualization session, remember to say, "All this, or something better, manifests for me now in the best possible way for all concerned." Then release the affirmation and let the universe go to work.

Give Thanks in Advance

And always thank the universe in advance for the abundance and prosperity you are about to receive, knowing that your dream will be realized at the perfect time and in the perfect way!

Activity C: Victory Celebration!

This activity, *Victory Celebration*, is an effective technique that reinforces your affirmations. You can use it anytime to make an affirmation or visualization session more powerful.

After you have fully imagined the scene as it is happening *in the present* and have made it real to your full satisfaction, move forward in your mind to a time shortly *after* your goal has been achieved.

Using the same technique as you just did in Activity B, *Living Your Dream*, visualize what is happening *just after* you have reached your goal. Are you celebrating with friends, family, or colleagues? Are you feeling elated, exhilarated, triumphant? Are you dancing a victory dance? Are people congratulating you?

And at the end of the day, are you crawling into bed with a smile and a full feeling of satisfaction and completion? Are you happy and at peace? In your imagination, watch your joyful reaction to your success.

Continue visualizing your victory celebration for several minutes or as long as you wish.

Remember, each time you finish any affirmation or visualization, release it with the confidence that the best possible outcome will be realized. Finish by saying, "All this, or something better, manifests for me now in the best possible way for all concerned." *Know* that this is true. Then, give thanks to the creative intelligence for co-creating this success with you, and fill your mind with gratitude for this wonderful gift.

Infinite worlds appear and disappear

in the vast expanse

of my own consciousness,

like motes of dust

dancing in a beam of light.

—*Ancient Vedic Saying*

Let the waters settle

you will see stars and moon

mirrored in your Being.

—Rumi

19.

Faith and Knowing

Have you ever had a hunch that you were absolutely certain was true? You had no external evidence of something, but somehow you were sure of it beyond the shadow of a doubt and later on you found out that your hunch was correct? This is the experience of *knowing*.

This energy of certainty can help your dreams manifest in the best way possible. *Knowing* that your prosperity is now real aligns you with all the abundance that is naturally a part of this universe and attracts it to you. You strengthen the feeling of *knowing* by developing an unshakable confidence within you that your dreams are real.

Prosperity and abundance *are* yours now because spiritual energy is everywhere and in everything, including you. Since spirit (or God) is abundant, loving, and extravagant by nature, you possess these qualities as well.

When you *know* that your dreams are coming true, you create an unstoppable energy within and around you that has everything to do with prosperity—expansiveness, abundance, limitlessness, and boundlessness—and you gently absorb these qualities. In a sense, you *become* prosperity. So say your affirmations with a strong sense of knowing that your personal prosperity is a real part of your life in this moment.

Prosperity Law #52

I Fuel My Dreams with Faith

After you do the footwork (goal setting, affirming, visualizing), your job is done. You must now hand over the controls to the creative force. This is faith in action.

Each time you finish your affirmations, give thanks in advance for the best possible outcomes; then release them. Do not concern yourself with when or how they will come about. Hold fast to your vision with the faith that the perfect manifestations will be realized, and do not get in the way by worrying or fretting or plotting.

If you are tempted to worry or doubt between affirmation sessions, choose to keep the faith persistently, stubbornly, and joyfully until you see your dreams come alive.

Our minds cannot comprehend the enormous power of the creative intelligence. Yet we can be sure that it keeps our highest good in mind. We must trust in this and step out of the way to let it do its work.

Faith is the fuel that drives your dream into manifestation.
After you've conceived a goal and completed
the preparatory steps, surrender your dream
to your higher power
with complete faith and knowledge
that you will realize the best possible outcome.

Activity: *Practicing Faith*

Use this activity when you are finished with an affirmation session or any time you are tempted to worry.

Place a symbol of your goal or dream into a small golden satchel; then imagine placing it in the beak of a beautiful dove.

Now release the bird into flight. In your mind's eye, watch the bird fly into the sky and soar away. See the dove traveling higher and higher with your golden satchel—up to where the creative intelligence will take control of your dreams.

As the bird disappears into the sky, joyfully release the goal (or goals) you placed in its beak. Then let go mentally and emotionally of your goal, knowing that it is in good hands.

Now is the time to exercise faith and to trust in your higher spiritual power. Always give thanks, and allow the universe to create your dreams at the right time and in the right way.

Whenever you think of your goal, just repeat your affirmations confidently, and continue to surrender your dreams to the best possible outcome. If you will allow it, the creative force will deliver to you the perfect manifestation of your dreams.

Describe your experience of this activity in your Prosperity Journal.

Prosperity Law #53

I Am Lovingly Persistent

When you are excited about creating a new goal in your life, you often want to see it appear right away. Sometimes your affirmations are answered quickly, and other times they may take longer. But remember,

God's delays are not God's denials.

Maybe a lesson needs to be learned before you can receive the highest blessings for your wish. Perhaps a situation needs to rearrange itself or a particular growth process needs to take place. At times, reasons unknown to you might cause a delay.

Even if you are feeling impatient, persist in doing your affirmations and visualizations, and hold fast to your dreams. Remember that the creative intelligence probably has a plan for you that is much greater than you originally imagined. This plan may need a certain amount of time to manifest in the perfect way. Allow for this possibility.

A strong trust in your higher spiritual power's presence and assistance in your life is vital. Be persistent in your unwavering faith.

Change can be swift; it can be gradual.
Be patient and consistent; you are bringing about change
in your life. Watch for positive signs of progress.
Persistence pays off.

Activity: *Persistence Pays*

By completing the activities in this book, you are in the process of accepting abundance and prosperity into your life. Suspend any anxiety that you may have at this time about manifesting your dreams. You are creating your life anew. Remember, the past does not equal the future. So forget about the past. Allow fresh energy to breathe new life into your dreams.

If there is an area in your life where you need to be patient but would like to see immediate results, try this activity:

Take a deep breath, and let go of any tension you may feel. Affirm to yourself that you have what you want. Relax, close your eyes, and see the situation exactly as you would like it to be. This might take time if you are holding tightly to an old image of difficulty.

Continue to perform this activity until you have neutralized the old impression and your new image has taken hold. If you persist, you will begin to relax and let go of old negative images. You will sense when this happens. You will feel confident, and impatience will drift away. You will clearly know that your good will appear at the right time and in the right way. Then give thanks to the universe for the fulfillment of your dream.

Practice this exercise now and any time you feel anxious or impatient about realizing a goal or an affirmation.

Record your experiences with this activity in your journal.

Prosperity Law #54
I Am Powerfully Silent

*Among my most prized possessions
are words I have never spoken.*
—Orson Scott Card

When we are excited about our dreams, we naturally want to tell others about them. But since everyone is not on the same path as we are, they may not understand. Some may warn you about being foolish because they themselves are too afraid to follow their dreams and they are projecting their fears onto you. Others may just doubt you. Others, still, may be envious, and these people will not be of much help, either. You don't want to allow anyone to "pop your bubble."

Being silent is a powerful way to help your dreams become real. The energy you use to tell others can take some of the charge out of the cosmic mechanism that propels you toward your dreams.

Share your dreams only with those you know will be supportive, but use discretion. Make sure you are not using *talking* as a substitute for *doing* or *be-ing*. We want to *create* our dreams, not just talk about them.

Use your energy and excitement to manifest your dreams; then you can openly share your joy and abundance with others.

*Telling others of the dreams that are closest to your heart
dissipates your energy.
Stay silent and inwardly focused,
and your secrets will become magic in motion.*

Activity: *Powerful Silence*

Next time you want to share your excitement about your dreams or goals with someone else (other than a supportive visualization partner), write about them in your prosperity journal instead.

Write about how happy you are to be moving toward your goal, and how excited you are about the progress you are making. Write down all the little details you might tell someone else.

Although talking about your goals to others is fun, this writing activity helps contain your enthusiasm within you and allows that positive energy to build and become a stronger magnetizing force.

Try this activity next time you feel that you *must tell someone* about your dreams, and watch your excitement and inner resolve grow stronger.

Prosperity Law #55

I Feel and Act as if What I Want Is Already So

Faithfully back up your goals with your actions and emotions throughout the day. Imagine that you already *are* the person you want to be. If you spend your time disbelieving that your desired outcome is possible, or feeling and acting negatively between affirmations, you are undoing your prosperity work.

Steadfastly remember your positive intentions and the *qualities* you want to bring into your life as a result of achieving your dreams. Practice experiencing the feelings of joy and achievement in the here and now.

When you desire a goal and visualize it, you cause that particular situation or circumstance to move toward you and to manifest in your life.

You are in the process of creating your desired reality out of an infinite number of possibilities. Act the role, and the universe will respond in kind.

In your daily life, play a game of prosperity.
Act, talk, think, and feel as if you already have what you desire.
Soon you will become the person you want to be,
and your desires will turn into reality.

Activity: *As If*

Choose a goal that is important to you, and ask yourself the following questions:

• How would the person who achieved this goal act?

 Confident? Self-assured? Dignified? Happy?

• What would this person feel like on the inside?

 Would she feel worthwhile, accomplished, and satisfied? Would she have a high sense of self-esteem and self-respect?

• What would this type of person be saying to herself?

 "I can easily do that" or "I am worthy of this" or "This will work out well"?

• What type of relationship would this person have with her higher spiritual power?

 Would she feel connected and grounded in her spirituality? Would she make choices from a spiritual point of reference?

• Would this person speak and think in terms of what is possible, or would her language be self-defeating?

 Keep your answers to these questions in mind throughout your day, and adopt these positive traits as your own. Try on the qualities in your mind and feelings first, and then in your actions.

Write your responses and observations from this activity in your Prosperity Journal.

The soul loves beauty.

But even more importantly,

the soul thrives on authenticity.

—*Paula M. Reeves*

20.

The Authentic Life

Pay attention first to who you are,
and then bring those qualities into all that you do.
—Unknown

Prosperity encompasses being happy and successful, doing what you love, having what you want, and serving others. But when asked to define *prosperity*, many people are likely to refer only to money.

True prosperity is not determined by the number of digits on your bank statement but by the happiness and satisfaction you feel within. We identify money with prosperity because we believe that money will somehow create the qualities in our lives that make us happy. This illusion is readily supported by the media and by commercials from companies wanting to sell us their products. Those companies want us to believe that if we just buy XYZ brand, we will finally find happiness. But we all know of materially rich and famous people who seem to have everything, yet they are still unhappy with life. This is a common scenario.

Here is a fundamental truth: *Your inner state of being determines your feelings, actions, and reactions to outer events.* You can try to adjust and manipulate your physical world, but that will not guarantee that you will experience the qualities *within you* that you want. To prepare your *Self* for total inner and outer prosperity, you must make sure that you are experiencing an excellent quality of life here in this moment, on all levels of being. That is why we now turn our focus to living with integrity.

Prosperity Law #56
I Align All Parts of My Being
and Live with Integrity

You create health and wealth in all areas of your life when you align and integrate your *mind, body, emotions, spirit, and creative essence* with one another. Integrity means honoring what is important to you in each of these areas. This is crucial if you wish to feel whole, complete, and satisfied.

If you choose to pursue a goal that conflicts negatively with any one of these five areas, or if you are being dishonest somehow, you are living out of integrity. This will cause an inner dissonance and will lower the life energy that helps you to create prosperity.

Being out of integrity also occurs in situations where your *feelings* tell you to do one thing, while your *intellect* wants you to do something else, and you act and speak in a way contrary to one or both. A frustrating skirmish develops within you while you try to decide which impulse to listen to. No matter what action you take, you end up feeling fragmented and unsatisfied.

For instance, perhaps you wish to make a lot of money at a job, but the job requires you to overcharge clients for services, overwork or underpay your employees, or cheat people in some other way. Maybe you are selling a product you don't believe in or one that is harmful to others or to the environment.

Situations such as these will create deep feelings of guilt and shame, and even an underlying distrust of others. The resulting negativity will steal your serenity and some of your energy, while causing you to feel drained and dissatisfied.

Because of this, you will ultimately be unable to hold yourself in high esteem, and you will be in conflict with your inner spirit.

If you are participating in some form of dishonesty, then you also do not trust the universe to support you in creating abundance. This trust is vital for a truly prosperous life.

When you are in harmony and in integrity with all five levels of being—mind, body, emotions, spirit, and creative essence—you will experience inner peace and alignment with your spiritual self, as well as your higher power.

Integration means clearing out the conflicts within you and aligning your different aspects. It resolves the inner battles that make you miserable. This is a profound and rewarding task with benefits that will last for your lifetime.*

*Aligning your mental, emotional, physical, spiritual, and creative selves manifests an inner sense of harmony that spills over into every part of your life.
For true prosperity, employ the same principles and standards of integrity across all aspects of your being.*

*A quick note: This section of *Secrets to Lifelong Prosperity* is an introduction to the deep-healing process of integration. If you would like to learn more about integration, read the book *The Hoffman Process: The World Famous Technique that Empowers You to Forgive Your Past, Heal Your Present, and Transform Your Future*, written by Tim Laurence. You may also wish to read a free article online called "The Negative Love Syndrome" at http://www.HoffmanInstitute.org/nls.html And see the home page of the Hoffman Institute Web site at http://www.HoffmanInstitute.org

Lock into Prosperity on All Levels of Being

Balance and alignment of your mind, body, spirit, emotion, and creative essence are important in effectively creating a life you truly love. The health of all five aspects is equally vital, as they are interrelated.

For example, our thoughts affect our emotions, and our emotions affect our thoughts. Physical illness affects both our emotions and our thoughts. Our spirit can also factor in. If we don't feel connected to our higher spiritual power, we may that our lives are empty and have no meaning.

Do you see how all five aspects are interconnected and equally need attention? An imbalance in one area will have an influence on all the others. *Below are some steps you can take to begin nurturing an inner harmony and integration now.*

Mentally: Think thoughts that are productive, prosperous, and uplifting. Work through and release negativity.

Physically: Take care of yourself by being relaxed, purposeful, and efficient. Consciously maintain good health.

Emotionally: Cultivate feelings of thankfulness, love, self-worth, forgiveness, and compassion. Resolve inner conflicts.

Spiritually: Connect regularly with your higher spiritual power; stay receptive to guidance. Live in the present.

Creatively: Discover and fully express your creative energies.

Prosperity, abundance, success, love, and joy are our natural states. If we are not regularly experiencing these states, a blockage or conflict exists somewhere. We must heal and release these problems to make room for prosperity on all levels of being.

Prosperity Law #57
I Take Care of My Physical Well Being and Strive Towards Balance and Serenity

Good air, food, and water, moderate exercise, and regular relaxation are all an integral part of prosperity. Without physical health, it is difficult to appreciate all the other wonderful things in your life. Health promotes joy and quality of life.

When we are taking care of our physical health, we often overlook the health of the mind and emotions. Most people are aware of the need for exercise, rest, and healthful food. But we don't often think about the fact that our mental and emotional states are intimately tied to our physical sense of well-being. Stress or worry, for instance, wears down your body and weakens your immune system. If you are feeling unhappy, unhealthy, fatigued, or anxious much of the day, it is time for an overall tune-up.

Tending to your mind, body, emotions, spirit, and creative essence is the key to health and true prosperity. This point may seem obvious to some people, but how many of us are successfully engaged in achieving this balancing act?

Evaluate each area of your life. The goal is to increase health on every level by gradually adding positive influences and subtracting negative influences. Take *action* to build total health.

Your body is the vehicle with which you experience the world.
Take care of your health on all levels; you will discover and
create more joy and prosperity within and without.
Your health is your greatest wealth.

A note about recurring negative thoughts or moods...
Some people continue to suffer from constant negative thoughts, anxiety, or blue moods, even though the rest of their lives seem to be in order. They spend years trying to make themselves think positively but without success. The problem may not lie mainly in their thinking habits but in their bodies. These people cannot feel happy or think positive thoughts no matter how hard they try. These symptoms are often caused by a physical condition commonly known as depression.

Many people are unaware that depression and other mood difficulties are sometimes due to a biochemical imbalance that can be inherited genetically or set off by acute stress. We often do not realize this problem is physiological because it feels more emotional than physical. "Positive thinking crashes and burns in the face of depression," according to Dr. Harold Bloomfield, author of the excellent book *How to Heal Depression*.

If you find that you cannot feel good even after properly attending to the health of all five aspects of your being, learn more about the condition that seems to apply to your particular set of symptoms by reading books and articles, and seek competent professional help if necessary. If you experience symptoms like depression, compulsive negative thinking, anxiety, or other unusual and uncomfortable feelings for a period longer than a couple of weeks, it would be wise, even essential, to get a checkup with a good doctor who *specializes* in healing the potential problems with talk therapy, nutrition, and possibly medication, if that is what your body requires to heal.

Some people are reluctant to admit that they cannot completely control their thoughts or moods. There is no reason to feel shame for having a condition that can be inherited genetically—just as diabetes is inherited. Just be sure to give yourself the care necessary to heal.

Activity: *What is your HQ—Health Quotient?*

What areas of your life need attention and healing right now? What do you need to add to your routine, what do you need to take away? We will now take stock of your life. *Write your responses to the following questions in your Prosperity Journal.*

· What are the choices you make on a regular basis that promote physical health? For example, eating fresh fruits and vegetables; quietly meditating; exercising; deep breathing; stretching.

· Pinpoint several choices you make on a regular basis that do not promote physical health. For example, drinking a lot of coffee or soft drinks; consuming overly processed foods and overindulging in foods that you know are unhealthful; smoking or drinking in excess.

· What are some changes you could make on a daily basis that would increase your health quotient? A good rule of thumb to remember is "everything in moderation." Gradually reduce negative habits, exchanging them for healthful habits.

Consider your well-being in the following areas:

· How would you rate your emotional well being? Are you frequently depressed, anxious, or agitated? Or are you usually relaxed, confident, and happy?

· How about your mental attitude. Do you worry a lot? Do you focus on the negative aspects of a situation? Do you complain a lot? Or is it easy for you to be positive?

· How connected do you feel to your higher spiritual power? Do you feel lovingly guided and protected, or disconnected?

· How creatively fulfilled are you? Do you feel challenged, ready for adventure? Are you fully utilizing and expressing your creative potential?

Each soul is potentially divine

and the goal is to manifest that divinity.

Everything else is secondary.

—George Harrison

21.

Healing Addiction

This chapter talks about a widespread problem in a few short pages. It is not meant to be a complete treatise on healing addiction but more of a reminder and perhaps a guidepost.

These pages point out an area of life that may need your attention and suggest a few possible paths in the direction of healing and joy.

"Addiction begins by looking for the right thing in the wrong place," says Deepak Chopra, M.D., in his book *Overcoming Addictions: The Spiritual Solution*. He asserts that most people are actually looking for joy and relief by using their drug of choice. But the true nature of joy, he explains, is "a return to the deep harmony of body, mind, and spirit that was yours at birth and that can be yours again. Once this joy has been recaptured, there is no need for stimulants, depressants, or anything else that must be bought, hidden, injected, inhaled, turned on or turned off."

It is vital to note that Dr. Chopra is not talking about legitimate medications taken for physical ailments, biochemical imbalances, or mental health. This refers only to unneeded drugs.

In this section we approach the topic of healing addiction from several angles. We observe that addictions can be a way to cover up pain, so we look for possible sources of the pain and ways to heal it. We also realize that a natural joy has been within our hearts all along, and we discover ways to bring it out again so we can fully experience our inner spirit.

Prosperity Law #58

I Release Unhealthful Behaviors and Dissolve Them into the Light

We live in a chaotic and unbalanced society where most of us endure large amounts of stress and sensory overload. This outer imbalance is reflected within our bodies and in our lives by illness, discord, anxiety, depression, dissatisfaction, and unhappiness. In response to these invasions, many of us turn to addictive substances and unhealthful behaviors, which help us to relax or distract us from our feelings and problems.

Although they make us feel better momentarily, addictions often change our body chemistry for the worse over a period of time. Eventually the "positive" effects wear down, leaving us emotionally and physically dependent. And while these substances and behaviors are harming our health, our problems remain unsolved.

When we stop addictive behaviors and move towards health, we can reveal the hidden source of the imbalance. Usually suppressed shame, anger, frustration, and loneliness play a part, along with the physical dependency. We also find that we can experience the joy we are searching for in the addictive behavior in much more profound ways by rediscovering our inner light.

Once we acknowledge and begin to heal the underlying factors involved in creating an addiction, we can take steps to bring our mind, body, and spirit back into harmony.

Unhealthful behaviors and addictions are a way of seeking joy and comfort. Find the fullness of your spirituality, and you will no longer need the addiction. Joy comes naturally from within when we are balanced and healthy.

Addictions and Spirituality

Many people use addictions as a substitute for true prosperity, happiness, and spiritual connection. When we participate in an addictive habit, we are often trying to distract ourselves from some form of discomfort and make ourselves feel better. But ultimately, we just end up self-medicating and not dealing with our underlying problems.

Instead of building a relationship with our higher spiritual selves, we end up making the addictive substance our "god" and avoiding the activities that can help us to heal and bring our lives into balance. The addiction becomes the answer to our unhappiness or discomfort, while our real problems go unsolved, and our spiritual needs go unanswered.

These underlying problems can include job-related stress or relationship difficulties. Negative thinking habits, suppressed emotions, and deep-rooted feelings of shame can also play a part, as can physical and biochemical imbalances. Any issue that we do not feel ready or able to confront can contribute to an addictive habit.

If you need to heal an addiction, explore the myriad options available for ending addictive behaviors and find the one that is right for you. Reinforce the healing process by strengthening your bond to your inner self and higher spiritual power, and by utilizing other effective methods to bring your life and body into balance (i.e., nutrition, exercise, meditation, and relaxation). You will begin to uncover inner strength and resources to help you make the changes you need.

The Truth About Addictions

Addiction is commonplace in our culture. Many people have some type of dependency, be it chemical or other. A person can be addicted to substances such as nicotine, alcohol, or other drugs, as well as to sugar, caffeine, or food in general. We can experience addictions to processes such as compulsive gambling, watching television, spending or shopping, working, cleaning, and exercising. We can also be addicted to emotions, people, relationships, adrenaline, sex, power, or just about anything else you can think of. An addiction is definitely a problem when it harms your health or interferes with your relationships, work, or other areas of your life.

A habit becomes an addiction when you can no longer control whether or not you participate. In other words, the habit is no longer a choice for you; it is something that you cannot do without.

If you do not think a habit or addiction is affecting your life in a negative way, notice how you feel before engaging in the habit. Are you feeling uncomfortable and seeking relief? This can be a sign that you are not addressing your problems and authentic feelings in a direct and honest way. *Once again, please note that this does not include medications that are legitimately needed for physical ailments, biochemical imbalances, or mental health.*

The famous line "I can quit anytime I want" is what many people tell themselves about their addictions. This is an area where rigorous honesty is necessary. Admitting that you have an addiction to something can be difficult to do. People are afraid and ashamed to admit that they are not in control.

It is essential not to make yourself feel guilty or to criticize yourself for any addictions. Accept yourself for all your foibles. Criticism does not help you change; it only makes change harder. Self-acceptance and self-love are paramount in overcoming addictions.

Addictions are sometimes unknowingly used to cover up the presence of a biochemical imbalance in the body. It is important to be aware of the possibility of a biochemical imbalance so that you can take steps to heal it. A biochemical imbalance can affect your moods, thoughts, physical sensations, and feelings, making stopping an addiction more difficult. Addictions can also aggravate an existing imbalance or even create an imbalance where there was none before. Keep all this in mind as you work on overcoming addiction, and take the appropriate steps to take care of yourself physically.

Information and help are available...

Information about medical and natural treatments to heal addiction, depression, and chemical imbalance is easy to find in libraries, in bookstores, and on the World-Wide Web. You can also use the Web to find a good specialist in your area of need.

Many excellent books and other resources on letting go of addiction are available too and can be the first step toward healing. Below are some suggestions. If you do need some form of help, go get it. The sooner, the better.

In his book *Overcoming Addictions*, Deepak Chopra, M.D., takes a positive spiritual approach to healing addiction.

John Bradshaw's book *Healing the Shame That Binds You* strikes at the heart of addiction, and John has published many other brilliant books, tapes, and videos on healing addiction.

Online at http://www.Rational.Org is a method of recovery that many people have also found effective.

Dr. Harold Bloomfield's book *How to Heal Depression* is excellent for those who may be suffering from depression.

Activity: *Recognizing Addiction*

Letting go of your addictions can lead to increased health, joy, satisfaction, spiritual connection, pleasure, and prosperity. *Ask yourself the following questions:*

· Do you notice any area in your life where addiction might be present?

· Are there any substances, habits, processes, emotions, or actions that you feel you may not have complete control over?

· Do you notice any underlying feelings of discomfort within that you would prefer not to deal with?

· Do you tend to distract yourself instead of sitting quietly and working through difficult situations, thoughts, or feelings?

· What are your feelings and attitudes about letting go of possible areas of addiction in your life?

· What area(s) of your life would improve if you were to let go of an addiction?

· What are some of the activities that gave you the feeling of pure joy and enchantment as a child?

Clearing out negativity, attending to all aspects of your physical and mental health, healing your emotional self, and adopting uplifting attitudes and habits are all helpful in your quest to release addictions. Be sure to consult competent professional help if you need to.

Resources abound for healing addictions, including doctors, counselors, therapists, recovery groups, and clinics that specialize in overcoming addictions. Referrals from satisfied clients are often a good way to find a specialist. If you choose to heal an addiction in your life, you are not alone.

Prosperity Law #59
I Move Ahead at an Accelerated Pace

Pessimism leads to weakness, optimism leads to power.
—William James

Even if you have held onto negative thinking patterns and other habits for a long time, you can still develop a fresh outlook. You can move ahead quickly to where you want to be by following steps such as those given in this program. The next chapters help you clear out negativity and make room for the positive.

Positive thoughts are ten times as powerful as negative thoughts. Feeling sincerely positive is invigorating, while being negative siphons away a great deal of energy. Your natural state is to be joyful and enthusiastic.

Think of a river. Swimming against the flow is more difficult than swimming with the flow. When you practice being positive, you are in the flow rather than fighting it.

Let your affirmations work for you. Keep a positive thought in your mind, and accept that it can easily be yours. Allow good to come to you without putting up resistance.

Allowing goes hand in hand with accepting; in other words, allow the change to occur, and accept your new prosperous reality.

If you are afraid that change will take a long time, remember
that the power of a positive thought is ten times the power
of a negative thought. This will help you to overcome
even a lifetime of negative thinking.

Activity: *Remembering the Future*

Practice this activity with a goal or dream you have been visualizing or something you would like to achieve. You can use it to boost the power and effectiveness of any visualization.

Imagine that you are standing next to a large tree. You reach down into the dirt and uncover an egg-shaped container. This is a time capsule which holds your positive future. You planted it a while back, and now it contains your completed goal.

You eagerly open the time capsule. You look in, see your victory, and you feel as though you have easily and swiftly moved ahead in time to witness your dream fully realized!

Take in the fact that you have achieved your dream. See all the fabulous details that signify to you that you have accomplished your goal. Watch yourself enjoying your well earned success, and feel the thrill of your triumph. Pat yourself on the back, and congratulate yourself for a job well done.

When you are finished, thank yourself right now for caring enough to take the time to visualize and create this marvelous time capsule, put it in the ground, do the footwork, and maintain it until the time came for your future self to uncover it! *Record your positive future in your Prosperity Journal.*

Your visualizations are future time capsules.

You don't need to be a new you,

but the real you.

—*Arthur Hammons*

Instead of searching
for what you do not have,
find out what it is
that you have never lost.

—Sri Nisargadatta Maharaj

22.

Clearing

You may have denied yourself things in the past because of what seemed to be lack of money, but it is not that simple. The main reasons that you do not already have the things that you desire have less to do with external circumstances and more to do with your belief system. Your attitudes about money and prosperity are helping to shape your life right now.

As you have seen, if you feel undeserving of riches or have other unresolved issues regarding prosperity, you will actually push abundance away from you. And if by some slim chance any kind of prosperity does find its way into your life, you will likely create a way to shuffle it right back out.

In the next few chapters, we focus on clearing negative energy from our lives. When your mind and body are free of negativity, positive thoughts and affirmations can easily flourish and come to life. In addition, the mental and emotional clarity will make your affirmations more powerful.

When you first focus on the positive, negative feelings often come to the fore. This is fine. We will make good use of this tendency by taking the opportunity to clear them out.

The Power of Belief

Earlier in this guidebook, we saw that society holds many beliefs that are not conducive to living a life of joyful abundance. We must now recognize how we may be harboring some of these common negative beliefs ourselves and how they may be holding us back. Then we will step up to a higher way of thinking.

In this section we are going to discuss how to identify, neutralize, and release negative thoughts, beliefs, and patterns that keep us from enjoying abundance and prosperity. We begin by uncovering what we learned while growing up— watching our parents and authority figures and adopting the traits and belief systems that we may currently have. After that, we will choose to keep the beliefs we want and to release those that no longer serve us.

Like Attracts Like

As we have seen, much of the universe is made up of energy. Every particle within it vibrates at a specific frequency. You yourself have an energy field. To a great extent, your self-image and your personal beliefs dictate the type of energy you are carrying within you. The field of energy within and around you magnetizes and attracts outer circumstances that correspond with its vibrations.

The energy you send into the universe will return to you one way or another, so be aware of your self-image, thoughts, beliefs, and emotions. For instance, if you send out anger or fear, you experience anger or fear. When you send out love and trust, you experience love and trust and attract more of the same. The next activities will help clear away negative energy and make room for the positive.

Activity A: *The Story of My Life*

Write your autobiography. Pay close attention to areas concerned with self-image, prosperity, happiness, health, wealth, and anything else that you feel is important. As you record your personal story, write down what your parents and other authority figures taught you through their words, actions, or emotions about life, money, and self-esteem.

What did you learn from your parents or authority figures about what you deserved? What was expected of you? How did they treat you? How did they make you feel about yourself? How did they feel about themselves? What was their view of the world? What were some of their favorite sayings regarding money? Record any significant events.

We are not blaming anyone, for they did the best they could with what they had. If they did not know how to love themselves, they couldn't teach us how to love ourselves. But we are looking into the past for clues because we must first become aware of our obstacles in order to move past them.

You can write the Reader's Digest version of your story (short and sweet), or you can take your time with this exercise and be thorough. The more work you put into the autobiography, the more benefit you will get from this activity. (However, it is better to write a quick autobiography than none at all.)

When you are finished, examine what you wrote. Try to decipher what your parents thought and believed, and what you think and believe now as a result.

Activity B: *Excavating Negative Beliefs*

Step One—Look over the autobiography you wrote, and on a separate piece of paper (not in your journal) make a list of your parents' negative beliefs about life. Consider all the areas we mentioned, including self-worth, happiness, money, health, spirituality, relationships, and any other topics of import to you.

Step Two—When you are done, write down what you currently tell yourself about these topics. If you have been honest with yourself, you will be able to see in these pages some of the reasons you are keeping prosperity away.

Step Three—Replace the negative thoughts and beliefs you've discovered with positive affirmations. If you need to, review the detailed instructions on how to write affirmations in Chapter 16 on page 203.

Example:

Negative thought: *I have to work really hard to make money.*

New positive belief: *I am now making money easily and effortlessly.*

Negative thought: *There's never enough.*

New positive belief: *I am surrounded by the abundance of the universe.*

Write the list of negative beliefs on a separate piece of paper, not in your Prosperity Journal, but be sure to record your positive affirmations in your journal when you are finished. If you have identified many negative beliefs that are similar, you may want to group them together and write one positive affirmation for each group. Or you may choose to go into more detail by answering each negative thought with a separate positive affirmation. Choose the method that is most effective for you. *Keep this list of negative thoughts and beliefs. We will use them in the next chapter.*

Activity C: *Self Talk*

Once you have transformed negative beliefs into positive affirmations, you are ready for this next step. This *Self Talk* activity helps to clear any resistance you may have to adopting a new positive belief. Try this now with one of the positive affirmations that you created in the last activity.

Take a loose piece of paper, and draw a line down the middle. On the left side, write a positive affirmation. Immediately after you write the positive affirmation, write any positive or negative thoughts on the right side of the page as they occur to you. Then go back and write your affirmation on the left side again, and keep recording negative thoughts on the right side as they come up.

Just write quickly without thinking too much. This way you will easily uncover any unconscious blocks to prosperity.

Below is an example:

Positive affirmation:	**Response:**
I am surrounded by abundance.	*Life is hard.*
I am surrounded by abundance.	*No, I'm not.*
I am surrounded by abundance.	*I'm not worthy.*

Keep writing until no more negative thoughts come to you. Now that you have let the negative side have its say, you can begin the process of letting go and allowing your positive thoughts and beliefs to take root. Do this activity with as many affirmations as you like. *Keep any pages with negative thoughts that you have; we will use them for an activity in Chapter 23: Releasing Negativity.*

In the midst of winter,
I finally learned that there was in me
an invincible summer.

—Albert Camus

23.

Releasing Negativity

When you first learned to drive a car, you gave the activity your full attention. You had to tell yourself what to do every step of the way. But eventually you were able to get into your car and drive with hardly a conscious thought. You may have even had the experience of blocking out, or forgetting, the fact that you were driving; while concentrating on something entirely unrelated, your subconscious mind carried out the task. When you arrived at your destination, you barely recalled the process of getting there.

Your subconscious mind drives your life in a similar fashion. It automatically carries out ideas that you repeatedly impress upon it with feeling, and these are what you experience in your life. That is why clearing out negative beliefs is so important and necessary. By letting go of negative beliefs and replacing them with positive beliefs, you change the patterns you are unconsciously expressing and transform your life. The more thorough you are with the activities identifying your negative beliefs, the more thorough your clearing will be.

Regularly employing the releasing tools given in this chapter maintains an open channel for prosperity and joy. The process is simple. Identify negative thoughts, habits, patterns, and beliefs. Release them physically, mentally, and emotionally. Then fill your entire being with radiant, positive energy, light, love, and affirmation.

Prosperity Law #60
I Easily Release Negativity from My Life

So far, we have focused on how we feel about life and prosperity, what we want to have in our lives, and what we want to release. Now we consider the bigger picture: that our higher power can help us make these changes. If we truly want to grow, to be a positive force on this planet, and to be of service to others, we will be aided by this spiritual energy for the highest good of all. All we need do is ask.

We begin this process by affirming to ourselves that this loving power is within and around us now. We ask for help by being willing to let go of negative thoughts and feelings—even if we don't think we know how to do that right now. Then we stay open and patiently allow good things to appear in our lives, confidently trusting the perfect timing of the universe.

Negativity clogs our system and makes it difficult to hold on to the positive. By being willing to let go of negativity, we make it easier for the creative force to work with us and through us. This release does not have to be a struggle. Our higher spiritual power is working overtime to make miracles happen in our lives.

Create a clear flow of energy throughout your body
by regularly letting go of negative thoughts and emotions.
Your power to allow good into your life works best
when unencumbered by negativity.

Garbage In, Garbage Out

There is an old computer term called G.I.G.O.—garbage in, garbage out. In other words, if you put nothing but garbage into your computer (or system), nothing but garbage will come out. In order to get positive results in life, you must first empty out the old garbage, and then fill your mind with nurturing ideas.

Many people get stuck in their patterns. No matter how hard they try, they cannot seem to let go of old worn-out habits that hold them back. This is so for many reasons: change can seem threatening; we are like a machine with well-worn parts making identical motions over and over again; we gain emotional security from keeping things the same; we are unwittingly modeling our parents or caregivers; or we just don't know how to let go. Whatever the reasons, old patterns can be hard to break.

Change begins first with becoming aware of what we want and don't want. Releasing negativity follows. We are going to let go of the old garbage that was put into our system and make room for new positive thoughts, habits, and energy.

On the following pages are some simple exercises for identifying and releasing a wide variety of negative emotions. Use them to help you experience the relief and freedom of letting go. *Remember: what you feel, you can heal.*

Activity A: *Excess Baggage*

Writing out the following lists will help you discover and discard excess baggage that you will not need on your prosperity journey. You will be making lists about everything that causes negative emotions.

Feel free to include people, situations, and things on your lists. If you have negativity around achieving any of your goals, include those emotions as well.

Do not write this list in your journal; use separate pieces of paper, and use as many pages as necessary. Begin each page with one of the following:

I AM ANGRY AT...

    I WORRY ABOUT...

        I FEEL AFRAID THAT...

            I FEEL GUILTY OF...

                I FEEL ASHAMED OF...

                    I AM SAD THAT...

Just list whatever comes to your mind. Do some stream-of-consciousness writing, where you write quickly and let it all spill out. Allow yourself time for this activity. Once you feel complete, take a few more moments to make sure that you included everything that is bothering you.

When you feel done with your lists, be ready to let go of all this excess baggage. This garbage gets in the way of your prosperity. You will no longer need it.

Activity B: *Identifying Roadblocks to Prosperity*

In the activities from past chapters, you uncovered negative thoughts and beliefs, and you wrote positive affirmations for them in your Prosperity Journal.

Now pull out all your pages of negative thoughts and beliefs that you have put aside from previous activities and gather them together.

If your lists are extensive, you may wish to create basic themes or headings to group together the thoughts and beliefs that are similar.

For example, one set of negative thoughts and beliefs could fit under the heading "Life is hard," while other dominant themes might be "Money is hard to come by" or "I'm not good enough."

If you need to categorize the negative beliefs, be sure to write the themes or categories on paper that is separate from your Prosperity Journal. When you are finished, you will have a comprehensive and tailored list of negative energy that is ripe for release.

We are identifying and naming this negativity first so that we can clear it out and finally let it go. Keep these pages to use in the upcoming activity for releasing negativity.

Activity C: *Things I No Longer Want or Need*

In private, make a list of everything you want to eliminate from your life. Be completely honest. Include situations, emotions, relationships, possessions, and health concerns. Be willing to let go of these things, and trust that something better will take their place. *Write this list on a sheet of paper that is separate from your Prosperity Journal.*

The process of letting go will help to bring forth a dramatic transformation in your life. You will be able to allow more wonderful new things into your life when the negativity is released.

Special Instructions: Complete activities A, B, and C — *Excess Baggage, Identifying Roadblocks to Prosperity,* and *Things I No Longer Want or Need*—in preparation for the next three releasing activities in this chapter.

When you have the time, perform the remaining exercises in this chapter (Activities D, E, F) all in one sitting, one immediately after another.

Important Note:

Below is a summary of benefits that you will receive from the following three activities. When you are finished reading these summaries, read entirely through Activities D, E, and F so that you are aware of what is coming next and so that you can select a special time and place to complete them all in the same session.

Activity D: *Out with the Old.* This takes you through the process of physically releasing negativity. Old negative energy gets stuck in the body and lingers on, creating tension and stress. By physically releasing this energy, you unblock your system and make it much easier for your new positive thoughts to take hold. With a clear mind, body, and heart, your prosperity affirmations and beliefs will have fertile ground in which to grow and flourish.

Activity E: *In with the New.* After you have purged old negative energy, you immediately want to fill your mind with positive thoughts and affirmations. The universe abhors a vacuum, and it will rush in to fill the space that has now been made empty. We must fill this empty space up with what we want; otherwise, the universe will just refill it with the negativity that was there before. In this step, you read and thoroughly absorb your positive affirmations to make the clearing effective and long lasting.

Activity F: *Walking in the Light.* In Activity D, you released old, dark, and heavy energy with a thorough cleansing. In Activity E, you filled your mind with your new positive affirmations and beliefs. In Activity F, you cement these changes with a beautiful meditation, sending light to all the corners within you that may have been dark before, leaving you with a feeling of peace.

Activity D: *Out with the Old*

This activity helps you purge old negative physical energy patterns that may be trapped in your body. Do it to the best of your ability, even if it seems uncomfortable at first. When you are done physically releasing negativity, you will find it is much easier to let go of negative thoughts and beliefs and to effectively replace them with positive thoughts. Feel the loving presence of your higher power and ask for help dissolving the negativity.

Now, gather your lists from activities A, B, and C in this chapter. These include the lists and summaries of old negative thoughts, beliefs, and emotions, as well as the things you no longer want in your life. Grab some nice big pillows to pound on (with gloves or a plastic bat), or you may prefer to use something else, like a punching bag, and find a time when you can be alone.

Place the lists in front of you, and think about how you are ready to release all that old garbage and the trouble it has caused. Allow the anger to build inside of you, and resolve to let it all go. When you are ready, tear up the lists and pound your anger into the pillows. If you wish, scream or yell into the pillows if that is possible where you are. As you are pounding, say, "I am letting go of..." and name all the things, thoughts, and beliefs that you are cleansing. This may feel strange at first, but try it, and do the best you can right now. Your higher power will help you release the sorrow, pain, and rage. *Know* that this will be replaced with positive, life-affirming energy.

The Well of Grief

Those who will not slip beneath
the still surface on the well of grief

turning downward through its black water
to the place we cannot breathe

will never know the source from which we drink,
the secret water, cold and clear,

nor find in the darkness glimmering
the small round coins
thrown by those who wished for something else.

—David Whyte

When you feel complete, see all the old negative energy draining into the ground and being accepted lovingly by the earth, which transforms it into positive energy. Then imagine a brilliant white light pouring into the top of your head, filling your entire body with unconditional love and compassion. *Do Activity E immediately afterward to reinforce the positive.*

Activity E: *In with the New*

Make sure you have your torn up lists of negative thoughts and beliefs in front of you. In a *separate* area nearby, place your lists of positive affirmations. Pause for a moment to become aware of your higher power's radiance within and around you, and soak up this loving and positive energy like a sponge.

Step One—You will now finish destroying all the papers that held your lists of negative thoughts and emotions. Throw them into the trash, flush or burn them (safely, in a metal container or the sink), or dispose of them in any way you like. As you are obliterating the lists, imagine any remaining negativity draining into the ground.

Confidently state, "I easily release these emotions, thoughts, and beliefs into the earth to be transformed, and I accept all of the positive energy and abundance of the universe into my life." Or say any statement of release that feels right to you. Silently ask your higher power to help you completely dissolve these old feelings, and imagine a loving white light filling you with compassion, radiance, and power.

Step Two—When you are finished disposing the negative beliefs, pick up the pages of your new positive beliefs. Get comfortable and center yourself. Take several deep and relaxing breaths. When you are ready, read your positive affirmations out loud to your higher power. As you read your affirmations, *feel* that they are your reality *now*. Experience the thrill and the joy of what you are creating.

Take your time with this exercise and soak in the positive energy. When you are finished, complete Activity F to lock into the positive energy flow that you have created. Activity F is a meditation of light that further connects and bonds you with your loving higher power.

Activity F: *Walking in the Light*

You are about to take a cleansing walk in the light. You have faced and released the dark places within, and you are now continuing the process of filling them with a radiant, healing white light. Read this meditation while you are relaxing.

Get comfortable, sit back, and relax. Breathe in deeply, hold the breath for three or four seconds, and then let the breath out. Repeat this process a few times. Allow any tension to melt out of your body. With each breath out, let go a bit more.

Imagine that you are now strolling serenely through a lush valley. You walk along rolling green hills as far as the eye can see. Beautiful red, yellow, blue, and purple wildflowers checker the hills, swaying in the light breeze. As you walk, you feel the sun shining down on you brightly, infusing you with its energy.

Suddenly, a concentrated beam of bright, beautiful light appears in front of you, illuminating every step you take. The light gently and lovingly guides you through this lush valley of flowers and sunshine.

As you stroll, you inhale deeply and breathe in the fresh air, feeling within you the beauty and excitement of this divine moment. You release your breath with a sigh, then let go and relax even more.

The light guides you up a hill, past the colorful wildflowers, and towards the blue, cloudless sky. When you get to the top of the hill, you find you're overlooking the valley. The view is amazing. You can see colorful rustic villages and green hills everywhere. The warm sun shines on you especially brightly up here. You sense that where you are now is perfect, and that you are always in the right place at the right time.

The light illuminating your path is a now steady beam at the top of the hill where you stand. Its radiant energy streams down from the blue sky. You desire to step completely into this brilliant light and surround yourself with its loving warmth. Looking up, you inhale a deep, long breath and take one step forward, fully into the light.

You now stand at the very top of the hill with your arms outstretched and your face turned towards the sun. You accept the light shining on your face, soaking into your being and flowing through every part of your body. You feel gratitude for all the beauty and light pouring over you right now. The light completely illuminates any darkness that may have been there before.

Everything around you is brighter and whiter. You see the world through the streams of light that surround you like pure rain or sparkling mist. You gratefully take in the light, sensing that it is a loving and compassionate energy, so radiant and beautiful that it is almost hard to look at.

You are now a channel for light and love in this world. The light flows through your body, down into your feet and into the ground, strengthening the earth, and strengthening your path upon it. You are now radiating the light. You are an ambassador of the light. You are part of the light, and the light is part of you. By living in the light, you heal yourself, and you help to heal those around you.

You walk back down into the lush, green meadow with confidence, feeling connected and triumphant, knowing that you and your higher spiritual self are one.

Maintaining Inner Peace, Joy, and Clarity

When you release negativity, you create a void. It is important to fill this void immediately with positive thoughts and energy on all levels. Below are some suggestions.

Mentally: feast on your positive thoughts and affirmations. Keep them nearby so that you can look at them often. Make sure you keep thinking about the things you want in your life, because what you focus on increases. **Note:** If any of the negative thoughts or feelings that you released arise at a later time, let go of them again by saying, "I have released this energy and now allow newer and better things into my life."

Emotionally: feel the excitement of the reality of each of your dreams and positive affirmations. Back your affirmations with a certainty; *know* that these dreams are coming true for you. Give yourself love and acceptance. Live exuberantly.

Physically: dance to music that makes you feel great. Stretch your arms up to the sky, and take in the positive energy of the universe. Take quiet walks in nature. Dance a jig. Hug a tree. Do things that make you happy. Take good care of your body. Make sure your environment is life affirming. Surround yourself with loving people and animals.

Creatively: find a favorite hobby that you loved as a child and give yourself time and permission to enjoy it. Sing out loud! Think of something you want to create, *and do it!*

Spiritually: stay aware that your higher self is always nearby guiding you toward love and prosperity. Close your eyes, and imagine brilliant light filling you from head to toe. Find or create visualization tapes that connect you with your spirit, and listen to them regularly to keep you in the flow.

As your release the things

you no longer love or use,

you call back to yourself parts of your spirit

that have been attached to them,

and attached to the emotional needs

and memories associated with those objects.

In so doing, you bring yourself

powerfully into the present time.

—Karen Kingston

24.

Circulation

Clutter is a sign of blocked energy. The more clutter you have in your living spaces, the harder it is for good energy to circulate. Clearing your surroundings and your world of clutter and excess baggage helps to increase your sense of serenity and makes way for abundance to flow into your life.

A cluttered environment can make it more difficult for you to think clearly, be productive, and even breathe freely. Your surroundings are a reflection of what is going on inside you, and clutter in your environment is a signal that clutter is within your mind.

Just as stagnant water becomes toxic, clutter and unneeded items block fresh, clean energy from coming into your life, creating a stagnant environment prone to toxic energy.

Pass your belongings on to others who may have more need for them than you. Think of the things that you will never use as energy that needs to circulate so that your living spaces can remain healthy and vital.

Prosperity Law #61
I Freely Circulate What I Have

Your surroundings send out a message to the universe. If you have a cluttered workspace or office, or closets and trunks filled with things that you never use, you are not leaving room for much else to enter. Where are you going to put new things when they come into your life?

Cleaning out your living spaces and releasing what you no longer need sends out a message that you trust that the right things will be here for you when you need them.

Taking good care of what you have is a form of gratitude; you are showing pride in and appreciation for your surroundings, and the universe will reward you with more good.

File away what you need, and let go of things that no longer serve you. Give them to others who could put them to better use. Trust that the universe will replace them with something better, in the perfect way and at the perfect time.

Cleaning up and clearing out your closets and surroundings
is a wonderful symbolic gesture that lets the universe
know you are ready to receive more abundance.
Let it go if you haven't worn it or used it in over a year, and
make room for newer and better things to come into your life.

Activity: *Cleaning Up*

Go to work to clean your surroundings. Go through your closets, refrigerator, desk, car, etc., and throw out or give away anything you no longer want or need. Then keep those surroundings clean.

Maintenance cleaning will help you avoid unmanageable messes once the initial cleaning is complete. As you let go of what you no longer want, you are signaling to the universe that you are ready for change: You are making room for the new life you are creating.

A note to secret slobs: Those of you who consider your surroundings absolutely clean but have your messes secretly stuffed away in closets or other areas—go ahead and clear out all that too.

Prosperity Law #62
I Mentally Release What I No Longer Want

We need to let go of the negativity in our minds just as we need to let go of clutter. Yet sometimes we grip our challenges with such mental tenacity that one would think we were holding on for dear life.

Many of us mull over our problems. The words churn endlessly through our minds, which act like uncontrollable and disobedient children whom we've allowed to run amuck. Nothing productive comes of this mental activity, just stress and tension.

Wouldn't it be nice if we could train our minds not to go off on these harmful tangents? Our lives would be much simpler if we were just able to release unwanted thoughts and situations. This is not to say that we should ignore important situations completely or sit in denial and pretend that they don't exist. We just don't want to ruminate any longer.

We're usually not doing ourselves any favors by repeatedly entertaining unpleasant or unhappy thoughts. We are best off spending our mental energies focusing on the good things we want in our lives. The next activity helps you to become vigilant regarding what you allow your mind to dwell on and fluent in the language of letting go.

You must let go of what you do not want in order
to make room for what you do want.
Removing your mental grip on circumstances
releases the energy necessary for change.
Declare silently or out loud that you now willingly release old
beliefs, situations, and relationships that no longer serve you.

Activity A: *Let go!*

We are letting go of negative thoughts and mental habits in favor of positive ones, and we want to reinforce the thorough cleansing that you performed in the last chapter. To continue to deflect negativity and tackle unwanted thoughts, use any or all of the following techniques.

- Old situations may feel comfortable, even though they may not serve you, so an affirmation about letting go can help with this step. When you have discovered something that your mind is holding onto that you want to release, remember the affirmation "I willingly let go of..." and name it. If you are not willing but would like to be, you may want to affirm that you are "willing to be willing" to let go.

- When you feel yourself holding on to a negative thought, take a deep breath and picture your mind letting go. Visualize a fist, opening up and releasing the problem or situation.

- You can also cancel out and stop thoughts from running tirelessly through your mind. The first method is to say, "Cancel-cancel" in your mind or out loud whenever you have a thought about something negative that you don't want in your life.

- Another method is called *Thought Stopping.* You simply say to yourself firmly, "Stop!" whenever you want to stop mulling over a thought. Always have a positive affirmation handy to replace any thoughts you are releasing.

Reminder: *If you still have difficulty letting go of negative thoughts although you've tried many techniques, you may want to reread the section on* Recurring Negative Thoughts or Moods *on page 236.*

Activity B: *Talk to the Hand*

Is there a person in your life who is somehow bothering you? Would you like to send him or her and the problem away easily? Try this visualization:

Sit back, relax, and imagine this person before you. He or she towers above you while looking down on you with a menacing grin. Notice what he is wearing. See the look on his face, hear the tone of his voice, and sense anything else about this person that dominates your awareness. How do you feel about this person? How does he act? What are you thinking?

Without warning, the person begins talking in a strange and hideous language. You see that his lips are moving, and he is shaking his crooked finger at you, but his loud booming voice steadily morphs into a high Mickey Mouse voice that is chattering away. You watch in amazement as black mouse ears start growing out of his head, and you see funny whiskers sprouting out from his now pointy black nose. Circus music starts playing in the background.

Next, this half-mouse, half-human wearing bright red shorts begins to shrink. The cartoon voice gets higher and higher, and the mouse creature starts jumping around, waving his arms in the air. As he becomes smaller, he is hopping frantically up and down. The color drains out of him and he turns a dull gray.

Now, hold the palm of your hand up to your mouth as if you were going to blow something off it, and watch the mouse creature shrink down to about three inches, settling right into your open palm. You can hardly hear him, as his voice becomes more and more faint. You gaze at him for a moment: how ridiculous this little cartoon mouse looks, with his high pitched squeal that is now barely audible.

You are amazed that this silly little thing ever bothered you. You see how insignificant and meaningless it really is. Say to him, "You are powerless to affect me."

Take in a deep breath; then let the breath out sharply, blowing the little mouse-person off your open palm. Watch as he flies far away, his arms flailing.

As you see the little mouse disappear swiftly over the horizon, you mentally let go of him and the problem, and you quietly, firmly, and joyfully say, "Good-bye," with a sense of closure, knowing that you can easily move forward.

After this activity, let go of thinking about this person. Allow the visualization to do its work. Lovingly release any thought of the situation, and know that the universe is solving it in the best possible way.

If you do happen to think of the person, just send love into the situation. Be confident that the perfect answer will reveal itself when the time is right. If you like, go back and do the "Walking in the Light" visualization on page 265 to reinforce your positive energy and inner strength.

The practice of forgiveness

is our most important contribution

to the healing of the world.

——*Marianne Williamson*

25.

The Practice of Forgiveness

I think you will agree, lack of forgiveness causes a great deal of pain in our world. Just think how much better off we would all be if people in positions of power could settle disagreements with forgiveness, understanding, and cooperation.

That is a nice thought. Now just think of how much happier you might be if you could let go of any anger, grudges, or resentments within your own heart.

Holding grudges against others causes us to harbor great amounts of negativity. It really doesn't change others; it just makes us unhappy. This is not a behavior that will magically go away once we have money. If we want true prosperity in our lives, we must learn and practice the art of forgiveness.

Many people think that forgiveness is an uncomfortable process in which you humble your soul before another. But forgiveness is actually very personal and happens within us. It is something we do for ourselves. The other person need not even know we have done it.

Forgiveness does not open you up for receiving more pain or abuse. On the contrary, it frees your energy so you can reclaim your power. When performed regularly, forgiveness transforms your life and, ultimately, our world.

Prosperity Law #63
I Am a Forgiving Person

The road to freedom is through the doorway of forgiveness
—Louise L. Hay

Refusing to forgive keeps us hanging on to resentments and recalling unhappy events. This blocks our prosperity. We may think we are standing up for ourselves by staying angry, but we are only keeping ourselves from experiencing inner peace.

It is natural to be angry at times. Anger is not bad. It gives us the energy to make necessary changes. Acknowledge the anger, and work through it constructively; then let it go before it poisons you or hurts others.

By holding grudges, we are admitting that a part of our lives is not under our control. We feel we have been slighted, and we stubbornly hold onto the pain. We are saying that a force other than our higher spiritual intelligence has power in our life—and it is the power to make us feel bad. This is giving another person far too much control over how we feel. Additionally, when we hold on to anger too long, we rob ourselves of the precious moments of life.

Practice forgiveness consistently. Do the following forgiveness exercises, and let go as best you can, leaving the rest of the healing to a higher power. Then go on with your prosperous life, focusing on love and joy.

Forgiveness is a key factor in prosperity.
When you refuse to forgive, you hurt yourself most of all.
Grudges and resentments block the flow of abundance
into your life. Choose to forgive on a daily basis.

Activity: *Forgiveness Writing Exercise*

Relationships are the looking glass into our own soul. When we heal our relationships with others, we also heal our relationship with ourselves, and we experience more freedom.

If a relationship with someone is bothering you, or if you are holding onto an especially tenacious grudge, try this forgiveness writing exercise.

Set aside a time when you can be alone to do this activity. Do not write this activity in your Prosperity Journal; use a separate piece of paper. *Always remember to begin and end any forgiveness activity by filling your mind, body, and spirit with light and love.*

Step One—Write down the name of a person who has upset you or hurt you. Note what is bothering you the most about him or her. How does she make you feel? If you can, communicate your feelings by writing an honest letter to her. Do not write this letter with the intention of sending it. Say everything you would really like to say to this person—get it all off your chest.

You can also do this step by looking into the mirror. Imagine this person in front of you, and tell her exactly how you feel. Laugh, cry, say it all.

Step Two—When you are completely finished and feel you have said everything either verbally, in writing, or both, close your eyes, and imagine this person is responding to you. Allow this person to tell you that she has heard you and that she understands you. She has listened to your concerns, and she knows how you feel. Let this person acknowledge your feelings and express her appropriate regret and apologies.

If it feels right, allow her to tell you the reason why she acted as she did. She too was probably hurt by someone at some point in her life, and perhaps this caused her to be unable to meet your needs or to harm you in some other way. Let her tell you of her own pain, and how sorry she is that it caused you pain as well.

Step Three—When the other person has finished speaking, and when you feel complete with this conversation—you have said everything you would like to say, and you have asked any questions you would like to ask—thank the person, and be willing to let go of the old resentments. If you wrote a letter, tear it up, and throw it away.

Step Four—Say out loud, "I forgive you, and I release you. You no longer have any hold on me. I am free now, and I set you free as well." Take a deep breath, and really feel yourself letting go. Ask your higher spiritual power for help in forgiving if you need it.

Step Five—Write down at least one good quality that this person has. From now on, when you think of this person, try to imagine him or her surrounded by a white light, and think about this positive attribute.

Perform this process with as many people as you would like. If you feel the need to repeat the procedure with the same person, do so. You can also use this technique with a person who is no longer living. This activity can be extremely liberating. You will find that your heart is much lighter.

Note: Since our outer world is a reflection of what is inside us, try looking honestly within yourself and asking where you may share similar characteristics. For example, if someone is critical and that irritates you, ask yourself if you are critical. Perhaps you criticize yourself a great deal without realizing it.

Forgiveness is something freely granted,
whether earned or deserved;
something lovingly offered
without thought of acknowledgment or return.

It is our way of mirroring the goodness
in the heart of a person
rather than raising up the harshness
of their actions. It allows us
to live in the sunlight of the present,
not the darkness of the past.

Forgiveness alone,
of all our human actions,
opens up the world to the miracle
of infinite possibility.

—*Ken Nerburn*

Forgiving Ourselves

We are often hardest on ourselves most of all, with a critical inner voice that sounds a lot like the voice of our parents, caregivers, or someone else who had authority over us. Because of this, many people find it difficult to forgive themselves.

Some people don't forgive themselves because they feel they need to be punished. Some are critical of themselves because they think it makes them stronger. Still others have learned that being hard on themselves is a way to stay humble or "in their place." And some feel inherently unworthy of forgiveness.

Withholding forgiveness from ourselves is like withholding love from ourselves. And when we don't forgive ourselves we are, in a large sense, robbing others of love as well, since we can only give love to others according to how much love we have for ourselves. Many of our difficulties would be easily lifted if we could each just learn to forgive ourselves.

You may think you cannot forgive yourself because you did the unforgivable. But is this really helping you now? Did you do the best you could at the time with what you had and what you knew? Is there something you can do now to take responsibility and repair the situation? Can you resolve to learn from your mistakes and act differently next time?

By forgiving ourselves, we are not just giving ourselves carte blanche to act any way we feel if it harms others. We are finally letting go of negative energy that holds us down in the darkness.

Once a person who has been holding grudges or resentments against herself becomes willing to forgive herself, she will feel as though a load has dropped from her; she will finally be able to smell the roses once again. And, she can take the energy she's released and use it to do good in our world.

Activity B: *Self-forgiveness and Compassion*

Loving ourselves is crucial. One of the main ways we love ourselves is to give up being critical of ourselves. And that includes forgiving ourselves. That critical voice inside our heads belongs to that of our inner parent or, in other words, our intellectual mind. And usually it is criticizing the inner child, or our emotional self. We must allow the critical parent in our minds to grant forgiveness and love to this sensitive child within us. By doing so we make peace with ourselves.

Find some time when you can be alone and uninterrupted. You will need a picture of yourself as a child, a notebook, and a pen. Play your favorite music that makes you relax.

Take a few moments to think about what you need to forgive yourself for. Then look into the child's eyes in the picture, and sense her innocence; all she really wants is your love. When you feel connected to her, write a note from your inner child's point of view. Tell the critical parent inside you how it hurts to be criticized harshly, how you are doing the best you can, and that you need her love and forgiveness to thrive.

When you are finished saying all that you need to say from your inner child's point of view, sit with those feelings for a few moments. Feel the love and compassion you have for this innocent child deep within you. Feel the forgiveness.

Then write a heartfelt reply from your inner parent. Tell your inner child that you love her and you forgive her. Tell her how sorry you are for all the pain she has withstood and how you want to support her and work with her in the future. Release any self-hatred or anger, and surrender any perceived character flaws to your higher power. Continue writing letters back and forth between the inner child and the adult until you feel at peace. This activity can be performed regularly.

If wholeness can be recognized by how it feels,

the appropriate feeling is fulfillment.

Anything that is deeply fulfilling gives a person

the sense of his own completeness.

If only for a moment, one reaches a state where

"I am" is enough, without cares,

without the craving for anything more.

One is content to live on life itself, just the air,

sunlight, trees, and sky.

One lacks for nothing.

Being here is the highest reward.

—Deepak Chopra

Staying Clear

> The practice of forgiveness is not only,
> or even primarily, a way of dealing with guilt.
> Instead, its central goal is to reconcile,
> to restore communion—with God,
> with one another, and with the whole of creation.
> —L. Gregory Jones

If you have worked through the activities in these chapters, a great burden will be lifted from your shoulders. You will feel clearer and more in command of your own destiny.

When you heal your inner-self, you help to resolve and clear outer situations and relationships that are bothering you or holding you back. Letting go of negativity and increasing your ability to love raises your personal vibration and expands your ability to attract prosperity.

As you continue to do your affirmations and build new habits that support a prosperous lifestyle, make clearing a daily practice, a gift to yourself. No one else dwells in your mind. You have the power to choose your own thoughts.

When you practice maintaining clarity in your everyday life, your affirmations will be easier to say, visualize, imagine, and manifest. With a clear and focused mind, you will create the beautiful life you've always imagined.

True prosperity is not something we create overnight.

In fact, it is not a fixed goal,

a place where we will finally arrive,

or a certain state that we will someday achieve.

It is an ongoing process of finding fulfillment

that continues to unfold

and deepen throughout our lives.

—Shakti Gawain

26.

The Final Chapter: Surrender

Footsteps

One night a woman had a dream. She was walking along the beach with God. Across the sky flashed scenes from her life. For each scene, she noticed two sets of footprints in the sand, one belonging to her and the other to God.

When the last scene of her life flashed before her, she looked back at the footprints in the sand. She noticed that many times along the path of her life there was only one set of footprints. She also noticed that it happened at the very lowest and saddest times in her life.

This really bothered her, and she questioned God about it: "Great Spirit, you said that once I decided to walk with you, you would walk with me all the way, but I have noticed that during the most difficult times in my life, there is only one set of footprints. I don't understand why, when I needed you most, you would leave me."

God replied, "My precious child, I love you and would never leave you during your times of trials and suffering. When you see only one set of footprints, it was then that I carried you."

—*Anonymous*

Prosperity Law #64
I Surrender to My Higher Power, Knowing That I Am Taken Care of

When you have set good intentions, taken right action, and devoted yourself to something to the best of your ability, it is time to give control of the outcome to the divine energy of the universe. Let go of anticipating a specific result, and let the universe deliver what is perfect for you at this time. The universe *is* taking care of you.

This act of surrender can bring you inner peace as you wait for the fruits of your efforts to appear. By surrendering, you can create a space for greater understanding of whatever comes your way. You can rest knowing that because you infused your efforts with love, the outcome will be perfect for you and your spiritual journey. The beautiful ritual of surrender is a gift of peace that you give your own heart.

If you have come from a place where you have offered your highest intention and you have put forth your best effort, you can easily surrender to the outcome. Everything is working out for your highest good.

To surrender, simply let go.
Focus your awareness on the God force in this moment.
Know that this force oversees your life.
Direct your attention to being in the present,
confident that all is well.

Good morning, this is God.

I will be handling all your problems today.

I will not need your help.

Have a great day.

Signed,

God

Activity A: *Surrender*

This is an activity that helps you discern between the actions you can take to manifest your dreams and those you can release to your higher power.

Take out a blank piece of paper. Write down the important things that you want to accomplish today or this week. Make this a list of tangible things that you can do to move closer to your goals.

For instance, if you are looking for a job, your list might include finding a new suit to wear to job interviews. You may wish to update your resume, brush up on interview skills, and explore companies with job openings that interest you. You can also include writing affirmations, listing the qualities you want in a job, and making time for visualization sessions. These are the things that you will write on this list.

When you are finished, open your Prosperity Journal, and write down the outcomes that you wish to manifest. This is a list for God. What do you want God to work on? What are you willing to receive as the fruits of your labor? List the things that you do not have ultimate control over, such as having the perfect employer call you for an interview or having a position open up at the perfect company. These are the things you surrender to your higher power for the best possible outcome to be realized.

Write these down in a special section of your Prosperity Journal, and let go of them. Then take action and be optimistic. Expect many little pleasant and unexpected surprises along the way, knowing you have done your best and surrendered the outcomes to God. Remember that you are open to "all this or something better" to appear in your life. Know that the perfect answers will be realized when the time is right.

Activity B: *Surrender Meditation*

I relax and fully let go of the outcome.

I put my trust in the hands of the divine.

I rest in the awareness that I have

taken the right action

and allow the universe to deliver

my rightful abundance.

I accept my good,

knowing that the infinite intelligence

within me and

all around me

holds the keys that unlock the

secrets to lifelong prosperity.

Salutation to the Dawn

Look to this day, for it is life,
The very life of life.

In its brief course lies all the realities
And verities of existence:

The bliss of growth,
The splendor of action,
the glory of power.

For yesterday is but a dream
And tomorrow is only a vision.

But today, well lived, makes every yesterday
A dream of happiness,
And every tomorrow a vision of hope.

Look well, therefore, to this day!

—*Sanskrit Proverb*

Holy Work

All this self-discovery leads each of us to doing our holy work on the planet. The creative force turns our desires into spiritual practice by giving us a dream that is bigger than we. On our way to realizing that dream, we discover that the only way to make the dream come true is in partnership with the creative intelligence. As we develop this relationship, we learn that the best and most efficient way to do things is with love in our hearts for the good of all. This is the most joyful path as well.

Finally, we learn to ask for guidance. We realize that it is not we who really know best. It is the creative intelligence, which made us all in the first place. We have only the small picture in mind, not the bird's-eye view of our higher spiritual power.

Our dreams are holy because when we follow them, we find that the creative intelligence has something much better in store for us than we could ever have imagined ourselves; we start out with our desires for a better life, and we discover the faith within ourselves to let the creative force do the directing and lead us to our higher purpose.

We learn to surrender and let go, and in return we receive everything. We learn to do the footwork and picture the best we can for ourselves and the planet; then we leave the final results up to this great spiritual force.

The creative intelligence never lets us down and will prove itself to us time and time again.

Treasure Island

The treasure has always been there
It is not hidden
But is only where certain people would look—at all
Thus it remains a secret to the rest

They say it's hidden—or buried
To still their invading thoughts

Some are calm and content
—Or at peace, in their words
Some are stirred and cloudy

But they are improving their vision
Of the island—Of themselves

—Keith Jarrett

We hope you enjoyed
Secrets to Lifelong Prosperity
(also known as the HAR-MONEY™ Guidebook).

For information on the HAR-MONEY™ Cards and the
forthcoming HAR-MONEY Prosperity Journal™,
as well as additional products and books,
Please contact:

Treasure Island Press
P.O. Box 6477
Portland, OR 97208
(800) 795-0770

or (503) 646-0608 (Outside the U.S.)

And visit our Web site at
www.HarmoneyCards.com

Please contact us by email, mail, or phone
if you would like to share your experiences
with *Secrets to Lifelong Prosperity* or
any of the HAR-MONEY™ products!

Recommended Reading

Comstock, Kani, and Marisa Thame. *Journey into Love: Ten Steps to Wholeness*. Ashland, OR: Willow Press, 2000.

Fisher, Mark. *The Instant Millionaire: A Tale of Wisdom and Wealth*. Novato, CA: New World Library, 1991.

Hay, Louise L. *You Can Heal Your Life*. Carlsbad, CA: Hay House, 1984.

Laurence, Tim. *The Hoffman Process: The World Famous Technique That Empowers You to Forgive Your Past, Heal Your Present, and Transform Your Future*. New York: Bantam, 2004.

Maisel, Eric. *Fearless Creating*, New York: G.P. Putnam's Sons, 1995.

Orman, Suze. *9 Steps to Financial Freedom: Practical and Spiritual Steps So You Can Stop Worrying*. New York: Three Rivers Press, 2000.

Rosenthal, Allen. *Your Mind the Magician*. Marina del Rey, CA: DeVorss & Co., 1991.

Tolle, Eckhart. *The Power of Now*. Novato, CA: New World Library, 1999.

Werner, Kenny. *Effortless Mastery*. New Albany, IN: Jamie Aebersold, 1996.

Life is like a treasure hunt
with a surprise at the ending.
The surprise is that you are the treasure.

—*Unknown*

Treasure **I**sland **P**ress

Home of the
HAR-MONEY™ *Cards*
and other Prosperity Classics

You can find *Secrets to Lifelong Prosperity,* the *Har-Money Cards,* and other Treasure Island Press products in your local bookstore. Or, use the quick order form below.

✎ **Telephone orders:** Call toll free 1-800-795-0770
(503) 646-0608 outside the U.S.

✎ **Online orders:** www.HarmoneyCards.com/order.htm

✎ **email orders:** orders@HarmoneyCards.com

✎ **Postal orders:** Treasure Island Press
P.O. Box 6477, Portland, OR 97208

Please send the following products. I understand that I may return them within 30 days for a full refund—for any reason.

_____

_____

_____

Please send more *Free* information on new books, cards, C.D.'s, and other products as they are released:

Name:_____

Address:_____

City:_____State:_____Zip:_____

email address:_____

Shipping by air:
U.S.: $5.00 for first product and $2.00 for each additional item.
International: $9.00 for first product and $3.00 for each additional product (estimate).

Credit Card: Visa   MasterCard   AMEX

Card Number:_____

Name on Card:_____Exp. Date:_____